THEY KNOW WHAT THEY'RE TALKING ABOUT

It's frightening but true: the men and women in this anthology were convicted of some of the most infamous and unsettling crimes of the century, yet not one of them remains unaware of their responsibilities to life and the world of the living.

Patricia Krenwinkel writes of the life of a girl in faded blue-jeans (Indifferent to cities/Open to Yosemite/With a heart that pumps a medley to the rhythms of life) and how that life turned into a nightmare.

Leslie Van Houten writes a raw story, of what happens when a cell block filled with women finds its basic needs unfulfilled, its passions ignored, its urges biologically bent. . . So honest it is bound to touch the heart.

Frank Earl Andrews has been serving a 55 to 67 year sentence for kidnapping and the wounding of a deputy sheriff. He introduces all of the writings he has compiled for PROSE AND CONS, and also writes a story of his boyhood—one in which few readers will not be able to recognize just a little bit of themselves.

Illustrated with original line drawings

Rahway State Prison by Othello Noel

PROSE AND CONS

EDITED BY

FRANK EARL ANDREWS

PYRAMID BOOKS ▲ NEW YORK

PROSE AND CONS

A PYRAMID BOOK

Pyramid edition published February 1976

ISBN 0-515-03881-4

Library of Congress Catalog Card Number: 75-42921

Printed in the United States of America

Pyramid Books are published by Pyramid Communications,
Inc. Its trademarks, consisting of the word "Pyramid" and the
portrayal of a pyramid, are registered in the United States
Patent Office.

Pyramid Communications, Inc., 919 Third Avenue, New York,
N.Y. 10022

TO:
Glen
Jane
Mr. Kren.
K.K.
Friday
Betsy
Dave
Karlene
Dad (smile)
&
fourscore more . . .
members of an orchestra . . .
whose theme song is *life* . . .

CONTENTS

PROSE AND CONS

PATRICIA KRENWINKEL—

California Institution for Women

Once under the death penalty, this fascinating woman was affected by the U.S. Supreme Court's decision to stop capital punishment, and that fact alone—that she was saved from extinction—makes the ruling worthwhile. Until a year or so ago, she was content to spend her time merely going through the motions, occasionally scribbling some of her thoughts on paper. About a year ago she was encouraged to send these writings to a friend, who each time came away with his heart in his mouth. She is currently involved in a journalism class and a law course, hoping one day to present her story to the world.

P.K. (A While Ago)

Eyes
double-lidded
round
disappearing whenever
a broad smile is formed.
Crowsfeet then
deepening with the seasons
grey
when wearing black
blue when accompanied by denims
a flick of green
in the forest.

Hunched shoulders
despite years of
"stand up straight"
scoldings from her mother.
Stolid steps
thick legs
lithe arms
stubby nails
once bitten on a daily basis
yet even when not nibbled upon
they fail to grow past the fingertips.
Feet
a huge success at obtaining callouses

that split
bleed
during the barefoot summer months.
Toes
incredibly liberated
each one moving of it's own volition
each on its own preferred course.

Daydreams
the usual worn-out
fantasies of love
Sir Lancelots.
Always finds older men
the most attractive
feeling comfortable
in their judgements.

Inadequate
to the latest styles
the newest crazes.
At ease
in conservative
wallpaper prints.
Daring on occasion
polish to fake fingernails
flashing a Virginia Slim
(coming a long way, baby)
that matches a violet
or hot pink outfit.
Embarrassed at wolf whistles
or emphatic compliments
delivered by better looking
but superficial people.
Will then take giant strides
to circle the "mode block"
where a return to faded jeans
armor-proofs
against pseudoism.

Indifferent
to cities.
Open to Yosemite
with a heart that pumps
a medley
to the rhythm of life.
A missionary for ecology
horny toads
gopher snakes
an empty lot
soon to be the site of a new housing project
a block of massive concrete
whose annual erosion
will not permit
the return of scuffed knees
running fancies
venturous
dangerous
expeditions into the unknown holes and nests.
Tends toward negative thoughts
butts
candy-wrappers
playing havoc with the beach sand.
An aide to needy squirrels
running to inform them
of her "Alice In Wonderland" scheme
but after the birds
take frightened flight
after the squirrels
scurry for scary cover
she will pull a weed
and say fffffffuuuuuucccccckkkkkIT!

Adores
listening to the intellectuals
angry that continued schooling
didn't broaden her perspective
quickly enough.
Sulks

in gloomy memories
suppressing meaningful things
she wants to say.
When finally given the soap box
cannot alter a stubborn opinion
even if later
she will concede to herself
that she was wrong.
Unafraid of diverse opinions
opposites
though angered because
she was unable to size up
that another could see her flaws.
When she is certain
that new acquaintances
will never be seen again
she will pull from her imagination
flowering up an event
to hide a mundane life.

Feels extremely capable
of doing anything
that any other human could do
but usually has to prepare
with a "go get um"
before moving forward.

Questioning
never afraid to ask
even the most direct questions
often times ones
that cannot be answered.
Immediately sorry
for placing one
in such a vulnerable position
eventually realizing
however
that the other's unassurance
brings a tiny satisfaction

a knowingness
that even kings and queens
have bitten their toenails
sucked thumbs
breathed air
wondered who they really were.

Sings loudly
in a bath
or shower
lathering in dreams
of Irving Berlin
Caruso
complimenting her vocal discharges.
After a thundering accolade
from the packed audience at Carnegie Hall
she becomes ecstatic
and encores with five more rounds
of row row row your boat.

Afraid
of being forgotten
during
after
life.
Willing to bluff it off
as unsensitive souls
approach a real woman.
Will walk casually
into a rest room
huddle in a corner
contemplate suicide
straighten her pants
rub cold water on her face
then return slowly to the world
smiling an excuse
for having taken
an excessive amount of time
to defecate.

Loving father
always being his daughter.
Loving mother
always being her daughter.
Yet
desperately wanting to be her own personality
free of reflective impressions
automatically accepted
unthoughtfully absorbed
by the human conditions
of a family structure
a universally appropriate monogomistic relationship
that forms the marriage institution
whose inevitable grand end
is divorce.

Finally alone
with herself
she will sit puppy-eyed
thinking it might be better
were she in a mental facility
building blocks
hugging stuffed teddy-bears.
She cries
at the thought of
having had to grow up.

Still Life by Patricia Krenwinkel

I Knew You Were Coming

I knew you were coming into my life
faith you might say.

During the youthful years
I sat on the sink facing the mirror
with the bathroom door locked
of course
just to stare.
Baby pudgy fleshed faced
gazing at the one in the glass
wondering which side of the reflector
the real me was on.
I always asked
"who am I"
but just the wide eyes and mused smile responded
as I jumped down
forgetting till another day
because the team was waiting
in the street
baseball and laughter.

I believe I was once a child
a formed and kneaded soul
made in the likeness of a million
zillion before me
small people placed in the position
of having to ask about life

but having asked are
referred to a new doll for the answers.
I, like all children,
had a new bike each year
and at home tv made me fall in love
with ever-new dreams
delivered by campbell soup cans
and ajax cleanser.

We grew thru the years
same schools
same christmas stocking stuffers
same easter basket fillers.
We stuck together out of fear
afraid tho we never spoke of it
exchanging shallow and superficial items
new dance steps
praising loud singers
debating philosophies that were soggy
with years of littered recycling.
We were killing each other
and after each "goodnight" I dreaded
making plans for tomorrow
because each time I looked further than the instant
there were always the same meaningless encounters.

I begged—friendless.
Oh, 'friends' we called ourselves
and we spent hours searching for new
exciting ways to say nothings to one another
ways to demean each other
while pulling out bottles of red mountain
over a barbecue
toasting with a cheer
"to us."

I was dying
and each corner of my apartment
my cage

was held together by a check
banked at a branch of america
giving me the convenience
of a new "twinkie" added to my shelf
next to the beans and tortillas
sometimes eggs
occasionally highlighted by a company picnic
which any respected corporation
offers its employees and their families
a policy to flirt
with the young upcoming presidents
an office to which everyone aspired.
Zero dollars a month
to park my car
spend a few hours on a crowded freeway
that always led home.
Awaiting there
the same mirror
the same sink
patiently viewing revlon's best
and the same face
asking questions.

Cold beach sand
a block from my apartment.
The nearer the water
the louder I spoke
free from others hearing
listening
as I paced restlessly
cursing into the infinite sea
which resounded and perpetually beat
as my own heart.

I struck at gawd
for his unnatural eden
which my parents had thrust me into
and reared me to expect

while at the same time forcing me to escape
my secluded neighborhood.

My supplications were engraved
atop the gray matter
under my skull
where I heard repetition
form the grooves deep
deep as my disillusioned self.

The ocean only angered me
because it answered my mind queries
in rattling jargon and pre-recorded ramblings
forcing me to punch a way through
its foreign words
alien yes
yet ceaseless with the responses

I knew you were coming into my life
faith you might say.

My need for you aligned
unnoticed with the patterns of our being.
Perhaps it was the evening quiet
that bent its ear
to my conscious prayer.

Away from mom and dad
away from the reflected face
a little older
a little thinner
but not really changed.

Your apartment
and a salute to days forecast for the future
perhaps a successful flight from bleakness.
"Hi" as an introduction
flooded rivers of thought
spilled into a different ocean

a new sea.
You became my walks
my talks alone
not replying as the tides
rather as a rain spilled down
from over the peak of my head
into my eyes
and then
my heart.
You bathed me
in a meeting of longing
but I didn't know how to act.
How does one respond
when an empty void becomes engulfed
by an intangible solid?
I fumbled
but the fumbling placed me in your notice
and your response moved stability within me
brought out familiarity
which had previously only been shared with self.

You reached behind the starving affection
called slowly
never prodding or coaxing.
I was eased to see
feeling safe as I fled the harmful quietude
I had shrouded myself in
for a swim in you.
I was bound tight
awkward
pleading.
It was written into you
and there was no need to speak.

We left
walked dimly lit streets a while
understanding
then under my roof
which would only shelter
my body for a day or two more.

Touch
your hands were warm against me
and I wanted you to love me.
I wanted thoughts turned into motion
I wanted to run
stand
fight
surrender.
I wanted to dispel perversions
customs
mores
multitudes of programmed sensations
that I felt should be mine
to accept or reject.

Perhaps a performance
make a play of it
be as the romantic fictional thoughts
that had bent my confusion into dreams
hopes that might lay themselves clean.
You knew and I
embarrassed
lay trembling
crying in your lap.
You ran your fingers through my hair
asking simply "do you want to make love?"
It was mysteriously quiet
and I felt certain you had heard
the rambling inhibitions
making their transitions within me.
You lifted my face with your hands
kissed my lips and brought forth
a calm "yes."

Rigid at first
but your hands began a dance
pouring heat thru me with your fingertips
removing a blouse

the remaining garbs
placing them at the foot of my bed.

Then you were bare
and my eyes crossed over you swiftly.
Adonis?
Apollo?
Mars?
No
Not even Paul Newman.
None of these were you
for you were *real*.
Your hair lay upon my neck
and from there you moved your tongue to my breasts
then rested your face
and listened to my heart beat
speeding to the summons of my nerve-ends.

You penetrated
not painfully
moreso letting it happen.
The blankets beneath me
previous holders of my muffled tears
now held our meeting.
I reached to assist
but with light pressure
you told me this was to be your motion.
Need was not a part
nor physical.
Holding to you
I gave up to experience.

I knew you were coming into my life
faith you might say.

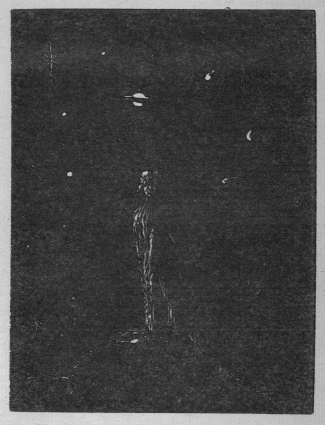

Othello Noel

Retrospect

City lights flicker
  green
    and
      red.
I wander into neon imagery
  and
    the pavement clicks
      beneath the heels of my shoes.
Stoney faces appear
  and
    disappear through doorways
  where
    frightened laughter rises
  from
    liqueur minds
      evolving ecology into sex.
I am alone
  companion only to the night
    and
      City lights flicker
        green
          and
            red.
Whirlpools of tarnished fluorescent automobiles
  glide under streetlamp beams
      a speeding
        screeching race
          to the stop signs.

A newspaper stand heralds
　　higher taxes
　　　political scandals
　　　　deaths
　　　　　a golf game
　　　　　and
　　　　　　　City lights flicker
　　　　　　　　green
　　　　　　　　　and
　　　　　　　　　　red.
Glassy stares
　　of drooling window-shoppers
　　　press against
　　　　　looking-glass candy stores
Billboards auction
　　a competition drive
　　　to the desperate desires
　　　　of luxury seekers.
I quicken my step.
A lost penny
　　confronts me
　　　on the sidewalk.
Picking it up
　　I toss it
　　　over my shoulder
　　　　and
　　　　　make a wish
　　　　　　for world peace.
City lights flicker
　　green
　　　and
　　　　red
　　　　　and
　　　　　　I walk on.

Frisco and the Child

Fog chills past any garment
penetrates
even insulated long johns.

Driving
vision is bleak
the hills become
an amusement park roller-coaster.
You don't know when you hit the top
only the bottom
Haight Street.

Walking
toes begin to ache
nose and ears
start feeling frostbitten.
Numerous faceless colors
leap from the mist
appearing
disappearing
moving snakelike
always evident
in
around
old concrete structures.
Love posters

staring from third eyes
hissing.

Nearby market places
joints on corners
puffing flowers
hash
grass
pipe smokers
coke sniffers
while the hypos
deliver their cunning so hard
you give a peso to their next fix
just to get them away.

Crash pads
incense and billowing tapestry
chimes and feathers
gaudy dance hall swingers
unwashed cowhands
spitting out slogans
impurities
while digesting a Big Mac.
Talk of freedoms
orating God
selling the devil
on prime time
sponsored by disillusioned seekers
floundering in parking lots.

Rip offs
run offs
jump offs
off the pigs.
The mass moves in daylight
which is a smokey gloom
of the growing end
near the conclusion
of the last chapter.
Blood is drawn

from any unable to move
out into space.
Reassurances of peace
as bodies are drug away
drugged
saved from being a drag
after O.D.'ing the night before.

Golden Gate Park
crowds mingling
in tempos
of the park tunes.
Musicians stationed under trees
suck in others
by playing haunting flutes
conga drums
that beat a mind into silence.
Dancing figures
in silks
gabardines
denim
cotton
move sporadically
jumping
pumping
innocent sexual
uninhibited grace
parading dreams-
upon the grassy mounds.
Senses enriched
the sun absorbed
into our eyes.
Clothes a nuisance
hiding the sameness.
The less we can get away with
the better.

We are the ones
outcasts of mores

built on isolation
together
speaking in acid
speed
peyote
sunshine
dopey crystal hazes.
Frolicking
with old childhood games
interweaving it
into the oneness of us all.
Hide and seek
amongst the knolls
laughing merry
spinning like a carousel
greetings neighbors
in heart
knowing we are open
feeling glad
for the wings.

Frisco and the child.
The world and me.

Him

Him . . .

Strumming
finger licking strings
that hum to a scream
the beat
ballad to a flamingo
home spun to sting.
To listen intently is a game
played around
your own mind's reasoning.

Nose a bit flattened at the tip
where it gives the smallest hint
of being broad
before streamlining down
into an upper lip.

His eyes ever constant
facial muscles moving
rapidly changing relatable expressions
but the eyes remain as a doe
friendly
aloof
reaching to the other side
making full circle around you.
Menacing glares when you step too close
without being invited.
Piercing and loving

you know he has seen
but is looking beyond you
and when he finally focuses
to a single sharp perspective
he pops a pimple upon your face.

Voice deep and calm
within the turbulence
of changing rhythms
repeating words
dangling as apples on a tree
prepared to fall
then caught like a fly ball
to left field.
You have the impression
you are playing with a dealer
whose deck is full.
You invite his words
while he meets your plays
and you continually ask for another card.
When he loses
he always comes out winner.
Defeat unspoken
in a past of unspeakables
understood
deciphered
when his eyes disappear.
Considering 28 years in walled cities
is unintelligable
to a coed cheerleader
of football reality.

Quick
tense
an almost detached stance
to his body.
He laughs when he knows you like him
and his mouth of thin lips
protrudes sexily

into a wide
shallow opening.
Relax and laugh
pat you on your back
walk away grinning.

Motion
hands forever mobile
if not on another
on his guitar
in his pockets
fumbling with a penny
a rock
a pen knife
flipping a deck of cards
like a mississippi riverboat gambler.
Always with dancing fingers
with a cig
running from and over the thumb
thru the forefinger
to the next and return
finally hiding it in a cupped hand
tho there is no wind.

Feet slightly haired
toes that clasp the dirt
like a friend
tho he usually wears shoes.
Top to top he walks
making the world his own
never refusing the day or night
his presence.
Moves with a clip
a shuffle
can cover an area of two feet
and make it into an acre.
Ballet steps
pushing sweat from his ducts
up
to be worn as the taste of life.

Works for change
but never repeats
except in a song
and even there
the music continues to change.
Makes ideas easy
for someone else to incorporate.

Stands before a mirror
practices as a comedian
on the grammar of muscles
and emotions.
Handles scenes
but exits when no one wants to talk.
Can make a show that will stun.

Sincere in fucking
controls your person
making sure you know
you have received a gift
and you know you have.
Fierce
never perverse
yet you wonder
if he even enjoyed you.
Finishes by lighting a cig
putting on his pants
walking away.

Never a thought about spending
$50 on a 1 lb. bag of sugar
nor a complaint about wanting salt.
Yet push
and he will push harder.
Impatient
full of drive
spanned by pressure
which he draws from
uses to his own advantage.

Sizes up a condition
how to move a mountain.
Finds the solution
buys a candy bar instead.

Man of a million faces
but always those eyes
which cause you to think.
He then tells you not to
"as you might get caught
unconsciously analyzing
a situation."

Him . . .

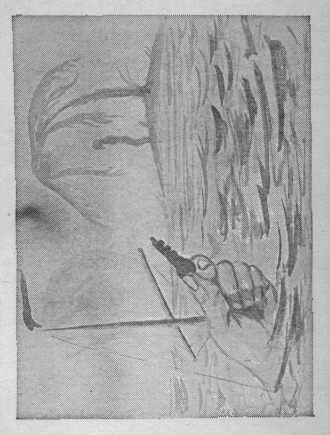

Othello Noel

Of Love

i watched your eyelids gently
falling as i lay beside you,
and beneath your chin, my head
rested listening to your beard
grow . . .

Waiting Rainbow

Rainbows wait
  right around the bend
    with patience mending
      the many color hues
        will declare our dreams
      soon.

Cold from Cold

Pregnant sky
  robed in silvery grays
    from departed blues.
I walk
  in sweatered body
    warm to your solid cold.
Nose and cheeks
  tight with frosted paleness
    breathy smoke rings
      rise to transparent light
        and the coat of winter
        gives birth.
Walking thru forest pine
  scented of fallen cone
    strong limbs stoic
      to the lacework adorning.
You are the first
  to be dressed
    of Natures' tatting
      beneath you
        my eyes strain
          to see your peaks.
Swimming clouds of white
  surround me.
I extend my tongue
  to taste the freshness
    of heaven and
      a snowflake melts
        into my eyebrow.

Othello Noel

Self

A game maze of networks
    tears and laughter
    joys and sorrows
The heart of love
    stirring the cauldron
    of
    flames
    where only the insane can reign
    brain train to be free
    making
    it
    be
    what I know
    as
    I
    fly thru the whole
Looking thru my eyes
    cigarettes and candy
    it's all a jive
Thoughts locked in perversion
    madness of words
    strangling the necks of innocents
    growing again
    into reflected perversions
All for one to stay alive
    I
    play

the
game
to
have something to do
In
me
is
what I see and do
My child
The earth run wild
Mother of Life and Warmth
　let
　me
　come again to your bosom
　and
　drink your sweet milk
　let
　me
　feel your loving arms around me
　only
　to
　see I am thee
World
　lost in despair
　the nectar flows
　in thoughts
　to bare
　　The Son of Sons
　　Lord of Light
　　　in flight free
　　　doves take the
　　　sky
　　　in winds soaring
Living womb
　birth and earth's
　giving and returning
　in circles of infinity
　everything beginning and
　ending together

forever wrapped in clocks
where time is hours
as if there were a meter of life
in living eternity
Freedom of minds' light
    I
    come
    and
    go
    into rays bursting stars
    Sweeping
    self clean
    I
    start again
The Garden
    while mighty minds
    destroy mighty minds
    thinking in their pasts
    never to know themselves
    locked in shallow grave
    made of selfish wanderings
    at glorious illusions
    running
    in fear of enfolding arms
    till words fall
    dead in the knowing
       . . . knowing is to awake
         to the Rising Sun
Into and out I come
    not more or less
    than it all
    grasses and beats
    I am God's
    power abounding in magick
When all was conceived
    in the spinning
    abyss of nothingness
    and woven patterns
    evolution

into
revolution
   and from the ashes
   open as a child running free
   bringing
   me
   home
The earth moves again
  naked
  eyes of eyes
  whirlpools of dreams
  reflecting
  sunny lizardly creatures awakening
  sandy mountains glorious stand
  to
  the thousands of years
  of
  Love's Heart
Being as it were and IS
  a mini spark
  in
  my minds' eye

       . . . me . . .

Fall In

within the confines of four walls . . . i pace . . . six steps
from bed to door . . . turn . . . six steps from door to bed
. . . six paces . . . one . . . two . . . three . . . four . . .
five . . . six . . . my feet keep the rhythm . . . my eyes
scour the brick . . . come to rest upon a spider . . . intri-
cate precision in a corner . . . she adds dimension to my
domain . . . six steps recapture my attention . . . one . . .
two . . . three . . . four . . five . . . six . . . an albert
einstein postage stamp glares at me . . . from a letter lying
on my table . . . his scowl is ridiculous so i wink at the paper face . . . advancing . . . one . . . two . . . three . . .
four . . . five . . . six . . . a word from within my mind is
formed . . . bites into raw thought . . . justice . . . just-ice
. . . just-us . . . just-is . . . is . . . is . . . just ain't . . .
the pace . . . one . . . two . . . three . . . body demands
interrupt . . . reposing upon the throne i ponder the plight
of any alligators or goldfish living inside the sewage lines
. . . a giggle . . . thinking perhaps at this very moment
. . . a reptile could be in the depths of the wet . . . con-
templating my fundament . . . i push the button . . . noti-
fying the ocean it can recapture itself . . . to the bubbling
rush i harmonize with three stanzas of gawd bliss ameri-
maid . . . again . . . one . . . two . . . three . . . four
. . . five . . . six . . . i am released from my cube king-
dom . . . to the exercise compound . . . meeting a friend
. . . we inspect each other . . . with empathetic eyes . . .
more pacing . . . one hundred steps defines the area . . .

walking on the inside brings the accounting to ninety . . .
together we converse on unborn dreams . . . sharing the
touch of hands . . . while we stroll . . . returning to my
diced container . . . i tighten my stride . . . one . . . two
. . . three . . . four . . . five . . . six . . . a kerneled question pops out of the popcorn machine . . . were i outside
my cell for more than four hours would i grow homesick
. . . unrestrained laughter breaks my pace . . . i fall in
hysterical disarray . . . upon the cot . . . sometime later
. . . burnt out mirth signals the call . . . to fall in . . .
pick up the pace . . . one . . . two . . . three . . . four
. . . five . . . six. . . six steps from door to bed . . . turn
. . . six steps from bed to door . . . i pace . . .

Best Foot Forward by Leslie van Houten

It's All In

Four walls and cold halls
   the game
   stripped bare
   and who's there . . .
Do I have to call your name?

I hear calls to guilty minds
   disguised
   they give up the guillotine
   in exchange for the electric chair.

Have they got your head already
   rehabilitation
   for living your life?

It is the perfect system
   piles of files and agents
   in numbers to keep the scheme.
We see the degree
   that civilization goes
   to keep
   the power green.

The trick is hate
   and caught within the net
   never underground
   we're picked off one by one.

Striking at one another
   another number
   or color
   the way you part your hair.

Hell, I don't care!
Just watching the show . . .

The steel billing
   (what's your feeling)
Step to the window
   admission
   out from the law
   a ticket from under
   have you checked it out
   it's a four-star rating.

The curtain draws back
   your thought
   I say, my soul
   what you holding onto
   the world
   that is inside these halls-walls?

Tier fears:
   step-spread
   what's up in your ass-hole?

Come on around
   and the screws in the machine
   hold it down.

How much further can you fall?

The wheel is dealing
   and the movie
   plays.

Liberals make you a star
   and the popcorn
   is free.

Strike
   fractions gripe
   new projectors
   film the mind.

Move
   on
   up
   clean
   put down.

High-sign the word.
This flick ain't so bad,
   letting the villain win . . .

FRANK WILLIAMS—

Rahway State Prison, New Jersey

Frank is serving a 65-year sentence, part of which came *after* he was incarcerated when he assaulted a prison guard. For some, that would be all they could see of this man with soul, but his writings display far more sensitivity than do any of his captors. Recently, he broke into print with a story that was included in a volume of prison writings, titled OVER THE WALL, which was published by Pyramid Publications in New York. He is currently working on a volume of essays and poetry, which he hopes to have published so that we all may have a chance to see the other face of Frank Williams.

the death of dirty red

the lock-up unit was unusually quiet. dirty red lay silent, listening as the night winds pried at the windows. before finally deciding to relax, he had read until his eyes grew heavy, and his back ached from hovering over his little makeshift table, which he had constructed himself out of a cardboard box. no furniture was allowed in the segregation unit.

his politics were the cause for him being locked down, but as he had so often explained to those who questioned his motives, that was the price of holding to and acting upon his convictions. one of the prison teachers, during a sojourn into the isolation unit, expressed once: "i think that people who die for a simpler belief are both irrational and foolish, quite stupid to endanger themselves for an intangible idea. i've been on several college campuses and those fine goals and causes always go right out the window at graduation time. everyone's interests turn to other fields of survival, mainly getting a good job."

red felt that the teacher, like so many college students, had no understanding of the meaning of sacrifice, that he and others like him couldn't possibly understand the plight of the grass-roots people, mainly because they never had nor would experience the same sense of desperation.

as he lay there in the dark, he thought of his heroes, men who lived and died for the commitments they had made and believed in; george jackson, frantz fanon, marx. these men embodied his revolutionary ideals and the very

thought of combat in the name of true freedom and liberation sent a cascading sensation up and down his spine. unlike george though, his dream was not to die in prison,
though his own eleven-year experience with one of amerika's eyesores made him well aware of what this beautiful
comrade must have gone through. therefore, he understood
clearly the danger of allowing one's self to be pushed too
far, and this was a constant threat, a threat which he kept
always in the forefront of his mind. he wanted to live, he
wanted the world to know through his actions that a grave
injustice had been done to him. unlike the thousands of other prisoners who passed through the manmade cages
around the world, he employed none of the avenues of escape, neither drowning himself in home-made wine or using
the various drugs that somehow had no trouble scaling the
cement walls. he needed no psychological band-aid and
wanted to make certain that he was in possession of a clear
head when every indignity, every insult, every act of violence against his person was purged on the battlefield. there,
and only there, would he feel the natural pride of a com-
batant. in fact, irregardless of the physical numbers against
him, the odds would be in his favor, because he was prepared to die for what he believed in, and this was something
the system could not cope with—a man who was prepared
to sacrifice himself!

further down the tier, he could hear the sound of a radio,
along with the subdued whispers of two men talking on the
tier below. the sound of keys jangling on a guard's side
dragged him from his thoughts, and so he listened quietly
to the faint sound of music drifting into his cell. the song
was a moldy-oldie, one of nostalgia, which touched a very
tender part of him. it was a tune brought to his attention by
his little daughter, "tie a yellow ribbon 'round the old oak
tree", and in his heart he felt that just she alone was worth
every sacrifice needed to re-shape the entire structure of the
world. there were times when he would simply stare at her
for long uninterrupted intervals, fighting down the urge to
swoop her small, fragile body up into his strong protecting
arms. in the instances when he did actually hold her, she

became shy and bashful, blushing as she melted like a snowflake in his arms. unbeknownst to her, her lovely innocence and honesty had taught him a valuable lesson of the heart.

hard experiences produce hard men. however, to become crazed with bitter and blinding hatred is a weakness, a weakness which he himself fell victim to. he had to defeat this, if there was any hope of making any sort of meaningful contribution to his little girl, and those millions of other little people who were now growing with her.

he had unwittingly let the years of prison life warp him, which was a feeling diametrically opposed to everything he loved and wanted to accomplish. he recalled vividly a conversation with the little one, where he explained that the revolution hadn't grown out of bitter hostility, but out of love. she was only seven years old, but already in her young life she had been introduced to racism, which was the main reason he had found it necessary to elucidate the principles of love and the revolution to her. she had been frightened and shaken when the guards first brought it to her attention that they thought it wrong for a white child to love a black man as her father.

it was just such incidents that caused the creation of the monster which haunted red's emotions and filled him with his obsessive hatred. most of the time he concealed and controlled his anger well. outwardly, he was mild, pleasant and courteous. inside, however, he was a walking time bomb with a fuse that constatly grew shorter. in the rare instances when the dam did break, his anger was uncontrollable.

many people hated him and even those he loved couldn't understand that dark side of him; or even his philosophy, marxism. there were times when his hate and anger cast him on an island of loneliness. yet it was his belief and philosophy that had rehabilitated him, made him capable of making contributions to his society. many sleepless nights had been spent studying the overall structure of his society, its economics, its social norms and mores, its politics, its means of production and reproduction. he studied with a passion and over the years a very clear and consistent philosophy made itself apparent. before this transition, he had been purely a glandular thinker, reactionary, motivated only by his emotions. it was during this period that he developed a raging hate for white people, a hatred within itself that prevented him from establishing any meaningful contact with those whites who might be able to alter his opinion of race. in the prison enviroment his contact with whites was usually an encounter with bigots and frauds, which only added to his already hostile attitude. when marx appeared in his life, along with rosa luxemburg, engels, lenin, che guevara, a conceptual miracle was worked for him.

dirty red had always scorned the idea of love at first sight. in fact, he had serious doubts about the existence of love at all. he had formerly believed, due to a tragic experience, that an intimate relationship of any sort was like moving through a nightmare, light years apart from reality. there was just no bonafide line of communication between people anymore, as if the age of automation had also invaded their hearts and heads. ten years of the harsh prison experience had only confirmed this train of thought, and they had been ten lonely and fruitless years, where the only thoughts that dominated his mind was contempt and hate for the brutal prison administrators. this was coupled with the same feelings for the wall of apathy tossed up by people in the free world. he fancied himself as existing in a void of non-affection, thrust far away from the heart of humanity. during these years he transferred all the love within him to one thought, one dream, one philosophy—the revolution!

odd the effect of a stranger's smile
her inquisitive disarming eyes, filled
with the innocent charms of youth.
we were both desperate men, handcuffed
and on our way to court for a charge
of vicious assault and battery
myself and a comrade of blackness.
we were sneered at, frowned upon and stared at

thus we found our comfort in the fact
that we were spectacles of frozen fear.
the horror showed in their white faces
whenever we came near. we were black animals
sent there from our chamber of darkness (prison).
there was no softness in our torn faces
and no doubt the residue of harsh experiences
lingered in our watchfuul eyes, but if so
she gave no sign of recognition
as she smiled her warm smile and approached us.
"hi there," she said
staring straight into our eyes
as i felt the earth move under my feet.
she was a friendly piece of a world
which had clawed at or forgotten us
but i could feel none of the previous coldness.

louise, contrary to everything he felt and thought, affected him like an A-bomb blast. she worked for a civil rights
organization that became involved with his case, once the
charge of assaulting a prison guard had been formalized.
instead of the slow, drawn-out process which he envisioned
as the seeding of any profound relationship, theirs caught
on like wildfire. after a few brief weeks he found himself
tremendously affected by the very thought of her. her being
seemed to reach into the terrible, empty places of his soul,
encompassing the entire lonely void that existed there. she
was like a tender shaft of sunlight, which left him senseless
with breathless rapture.

she wasn't as political as he would have liked, but she did
portray a willing eagerness to learn. this was only another
of her million and one attributes. she was outrageously
open and gentle, with a kind of looseness that made her
seem as free as the wind on a balmy day. he had always
been attracted to this type of simplicity, for it was a rare
quality that had been swallowed up by the corruptness of
civilization.

eyes strained and aching

as fixedly i stare
out upon the desert of night
seeing only those images
which scamper from the shadows
of my loneliness.
the dazzling networks
of prison lights
screaming out across the dark
tarred and concrete expansions
of highways
produces pains of distance
almost impossible to bear . . .
to the end-most horizon
of soul's dimension
your photograph before me
fills me with terrible longings.
i have come to love you desperately
it's as simple
and profound as that.

racism is probably more apparent in prison than anywhere in amerika, therefore the relationship of dirty red
and lousie was doomed from the start. the institution's first
reaction was to deny them visiting rights, under the guise of
an assortment of technical foul-ups and red tape. when that
failed to frustrate the romance, the interference was transferred to the mail, their only source of communication. it
took nearly six months of legal action before they were allowed visiting rights. when the prison officials discovered
that they couldn't discourage them anymore through this
course of action, they began to blatanly attack louise ver-
bally whenever she did come. it was a terrifying experience
for both of them constantly charged with tension and bitterness.

dirty red could have coped with it much easier if the at-
tacks had been directed at him, as louise had nothing to do
with the battle between himself and the guards. his war involved the world behind the walls, while they carried it out
into the streets, affecting those he had come to love.

Othello Noel

the relationship lasted for two stormy years and when it ended, it ended abruptly, with much bitterness and pain. louise had previously gone through two marriages, the last one ending only two months before she met red. she was left alone with two small girls, one from each marriage, and was searching for something to fill the empty space in her life, a void which the association even with dirty red could not fill. she ran through all of his close friends and comrades and each time one of them was released or paroled, they would go to her under the pretense of wanting to help him. always she would sleep with them, until eventually her bedroom activities became common knowledge throughout the prison. this provided his enemies with ammunition and the guards never missed an opportunity to laugh in his face. still, he persevered, realizing that the very fact they despised him so was because they feared him and what he stood for.

on several occasions he spoke to louise about her sexual behavior, but no words seemed to have any effect on her. usually these discussions only ended up in bitter arguments and nothing was ever accomplished. she even slept with his attorney, and this developed into a touchy situation, because every time the lawyer mentioned her name red would cringe. he couldn't even look his lawyer in the eye and he despised this course of action because it robbed him of the opportunity to talk about his woman with pride. he knew the upstanding member of the bar would be able to see through anything good he might say about her.

red continually tried to rationalize the situation. he would explain to her the spiritual importance of love, always praying that some of what he said would sink in and slow her down. he ultimately hoped to convince her that sex was a poor substitute for feelings of the heart. she paid him no mind, however, and continued to move from one affair to another.

before he had met louise, there was a great deal of talk about white women from his friends, none of it good. shabid, one of red's closest friends and comrades, tried to pound it in, despite the fact that louise also expressed a sexual attraction for him. as much as he hated hearing the things shabid said about her, he was forced to recognize at least part of the truth. the real tragedy was the admission to himself that he had made a horrible error in judgment, for louise was none of the wonderful things he had first thought her to be. somehow though, through a great deal of effort, he managed to survive the pain. still, there were times when the agony of her promiscuity inflicted a cancer-type eating of the brain. in these instances he usually ended up in a complete state of misery for several days.

louise's romances were always short-lived affairs, and he could tell whenever she became involved again, because each time her affection for him decreased to practically nothing. one of the thoughts that helped him to endure these periods was the feeling that if he had been free, there with her, she would have no need of other men in her life.

her final affair crushed him completely, for she made a clean break and the dude moved in with her. there is nothing in life more cruel than a cold farewell from someone you love.

"red?" shabid called from the tier above. "you awake?"

"yeah," dirty red replied, sitting up on the side of the bed. "what's happening?"

"you doing anything?" shabid asked.

"naw, just thinking."

"oh . . . you were so quiet down there, i thought you was either reading or sleeping. what was you thinking about?"

"louise . . ."

shabid sighed loudly. "damn, man! ain't you had enough of that bitch yet? she's a pig, a tramp and you know it! so why you go on torturing yourself? as far as she is concerned, you are a piece of shit, a gob of mud. she's a bourgeois whore, out for a little fun and excitement, a dance in the mud. that's all you ever meant to her . . . you was her dance in the mud . . ."

"i love her, man, and that's the only thing i do know at

the moment. a whole lot of name-calling can't change it. sure, i know she's a bitch, but i'm trapped, and i don't expect you to understand that."

"i don't understand, you say?" shabid's voice rose in anger. "shit, i'm the one who warned you at the beginning! i'm the one who told her you were my comrade and that i didn't want her to hurt you! i knew this would happen! i knew she would destroy you! you say you are a true revolutionary? Where is the love for the little kid a pig shot up in harlem? what about the brothers at attica? what about *your* people? has she made you forget your committments, everything we are both about! red, i love you, man! don't let this happen! forget the bitch! she never meant you any good! motherfuckers like her never mean anybody any good, not even themselves! she's caused too much damage between comrades already, and now she has succeeded in isolating you from the ones who really are in your corner —ones who will die for you! a white woman isn't supposed to be able to penetrate us that easily, but white or black, our women must represent more than just the ordinary housewife. they are also comrades in the struggle, prepared to endure and sacrifice just like their men. she can't possibly identify with our kind of desperation. find yourself a sister, a black woman, who could easily understand what we were all about. that bitch ain't going to make any sacrifices! believe that, man! Believe that, please!"

dirty red took a deep breath before answering. "i know you are right, shabid. is that what you want to hear? what i felt and feel for louise can't be erased in a day. it doesn't mean, however, that i have stopped functioning. revolution is a way of life for me now, the only life i know, and i will always keep on with the struggle. you'll just have to give me some time to get my head together. is that too much to ask?"

"damn, man!" shabid scoffed. "she's making you weak and you can't afford any weaknesses, because her people are out to chew your black ass up! you can't dig that?"

"look, shabid," dirty red spoke evenly, "all of her faults

are out front, but right now it doesn't alter the way i feel.
it's going to take some time . . ."

"aw, man, fuck it! i'm going to lay down! you sound like
a fourteen carat uncle tom!"

dirty red said no more. he rose and began to pace back
and forth, then moved to the barred door and stared blindly
out the window, across the corridor from his cell. a hushed
silence had fallen over the lock-up unit, a serene stillness,
which gradually began to draw him into the specter of its
tranquility. outside, the night was motionless, like a cold,
charcoal, dream-devouring monster.

words without motion
without swerves of action and activity
in time gather moss. with us
even the body language of i love you
has disappeared.
love is a thief
if you open your heart
which will invariably steal
the majesty and tolerance
of life/everything
every small joy
wisp of laughter
leaving only the terrible gloom
the immense emptiness
of her absence
i came
with not as much as a fig leaf between us
but having revealed my nakedness
she could not resist
her instincts
to prey upon my vulnerability.

tears filled dirty red's eyes, as he fought down the urge to
scream his pain at the top of his lungs. he cried for a variety of reasons, but mainly because he knew that the emo-
tional side of him would have to be executed. there was no

other way to survive the ruthlessness of the planet. the next time he thought about louise, it was without emotion. he wondered if she would ever know of her crime . . . murder one!

your memory exquisite
touches my depths
in a radiance of
soft tender pleasure.
i will carry you like a treasure
in my most secret thoughts
with the pain of your absence
to haunt the lonely nights.
nights that whisper of silence
the sweet lure of death.
i rationalize nothing
the right or wrong of it
and so i rise out of sleep
with an aching numbness
unable to hate your treachery.

Othello Noel

a frustrated revolutionary

i am the epitome
of a frustrated revolutionary
for i have fought
far too many battles alone
the apathy of society
striking the most stinging blows.

in silence without applause
i have won my tiny victories
without the concern of others
suffering my most agonizing defeats
while clinging dearly to the rhetorics
which went no deeper
than some hustlers pocket
who playing pimp games
could care less
for humanity's woes.

i am the epitome
of an outraged sadness
the creation of silence
and bitter indifference.
in a sense i am attica
which on the third day arose
a self-seeking individualist
untouched any more
with the world's tears because
no one has ever wept for me.

i am the epitome
of a revolutionary sincerity
which has slowly crumbled in the face
of my comrade . . . hypocrisy . . .

society will never make
another george jackson out of me
so that after i am dead
they can pick pro and con
through my death wounds
without the balls to live up to
prison and other reforms.

time

time enough for sadness
a wisp of laughter and always
time enough to die
time enough for love
the thin thread of a dream
that never came true and always
time enough to die.
time for a walk in spring
and the thirsty frowns
of a manchild and always
time enough to die.

and now the state contrives
a new concoction
a device designed to play
on the will to live
time that tortures before
it ultimately kills.

time that becomes a chamber
of endless night
and the sun outside a prison window
appears to thrive on sadness
time that is loneliness
and grows into madness.

o this weird formula
this bizarre invention
this design of the state
to murder with grief
against the protesting will
to live at all costs
tho there is no other fate
save to comply
to a reduced life of suffering
but always
time enough to die

who will remember quyyum?

for those whom your presence touched
for those who knew and loved you most
you were known as and called the general
and so you were
for these are times which should
make hannibals of all black men.

still i remember your smile
the times when our wretched conditions
would permit a joke or two.
i remember the breathless adoration
which claimed your trembling voice
in your elucidations of black love.

those were the times
we laughed and dreamed and plotted and suffered
in our prison within a prison (segregation)
now you're dead.

i remember the horrible news and later
the shocking impact
of knowing one or more of those
who you loved the most
had betrayed you.

i remember the numb confusion
which took hold of my thoughts

the pain of my loneliness
delayed but terrible in coming.
i loved you
almost too much for tears.

but because our cause is outlawed
your legend dear comrade
(brave and daring seeker of justice)
must go unsung, a legend
that turns sour in the mouths of cowards
cowards who will creep through life
on bended knees.

who will remember
this proud and arrogant warrior
too selfless, too other-directed
to turn a deaf ear
to the sufferings of his people?

who will remember his legend
an outlaw, a criminal, a male antigone
who aspired to a greater law
the law to which he gave his life?

who will remember
the courage it took to attempt
the righting of a wrong so terrible
that it engulfed a whole people into
it's vicious jaws?

who will remember quyyum?

ARTHUR DEVLIN—

State Correctional Institution, Norfolk, Massachusets

Art is not new to the literary scene, and his writings have appeared in various publications around the United States. His most recent accomplishments were displayed in a national prison anthology and he is back in PROSE AND CONS by popular demand. Art has been incarcerated over 19 years, and his main hope is to one day walk free again, before he needs a wheelchair.

SCREW

Should you expect me to react to you
As man to man, when every night your key
Locks my cage door and sends a shudder through
My soul, and makes an animal of me?

Should you expect a smile, a friendly nod
Of pleasant greeting in the morning when
You come and turn me loose—a khaki God
Who'll later only lock me up again?

And in your day's safari through this steel
And concrete jungle, should you not expect
The hunted to turn hunter? Should you feel
Safe or stalked by the ones that you reject?

Life is not a bowl of cherries, it's years
And years and years and years behind these walls.
But gates that close swing open, and no tears
Will stop the payment when the Piper calls.

WARNING!

Tiger! Tiger! burning bright
In the forests of the night,
Watch out for Smokey the Bear, man,
He don't go for that shit!

In mate by A.O.A.

BUT FIRST . . .

Reeeeeeeeeeeeeeeeeeeeeeeeeeee
 eeeeeeeeeeeeeeeeeeeeeeeeeeeeeeeee.
This has been a Test Alert.
During a national emergency
   all regularly scheduled programing
   — will cease.
You will be instructed
   to turn your dial
      to either one of the two special stations
         which will broadcast
            Civil Defense Instructions.
If this had been an actual emergency,
   you would all be dead.

PERSPECTIVE

I found it on a table
    in the prison library,
        in one of the many books
            donated to the Joint
                by some Square John
                    who cared.
It was a paperback edition
    of a 1937 Agatha Christie work:
        Poirot Loses A Client.
When I read the "Dedication",
    I was sorry I'd bothered.
        "TO DEAR PETER
        Most faithful of friends
        and dearest of companions,
        a dog in a thousand."
A dog.
The book was dedicated
    to a *dog!*
Right then,
    I knew how unimportant
        I really was
            in the scheme of things.

NIGHT BEAT

I guess
   the rule
      is just one of prison's imponderables.
If the Night Checker
   catches you masturbating,
      they solve the problem
         by removing you from your cell
            and putting you on Third Floor Isolation
            as punishment.
One of these days
   it's going to dawn on them
      that you take your pecker with you.

PROFESSIONAL MOURNERS

For money,
   they falsely weep
      and moan
         and beat their breasts
            at a stranger's funeral.
What do they do
   when someone *they* loves dies?
To prove their sorrow
   to their friends,
      must they force themselves
         to laugh?

Othello Noel

CHARLIE

What a ballbuster!
Fifteen years of waiting.
Fifteen long years
  of sweating it out,
    day after day,
      in this motherfucking mausoleum
        they call a prison.
And when you've finally made it,
  a Parole—
     28 days and a "get-up"—
      they check out your asshole
       and find you have cancer.
Jesus H. Chrsit!
How long were you shitting blood
  before you finally told them about it?
You with the genius I.Q.
  and the brain that comes along
    maybe once in a hundred years.
You could tell them
  the names of King Lear's three daughters,
    the number of zeroes in a googolplex,
      who invented the safety pin,
        what Mendel did with those garden peas,
        and why stars twinkle.
But you couldn't tell them about your asshole
  until it was too late.

So now you've done your Life bit
and you're serving out your last sentence.
Three months, they say.
Maybe six.
A year, if you're lucky.
It makes me stop and wonder.
How many fucking judges are there?

LINDA HAINES—

California Institution for Women

This beautiful lady is a perfect example of the "gold" we bury in our prisons. She has been down several years on a life sentence, but hasn't permitted herself to stagnate. Linda can write, paint, sing and brighten up a room just by being there. Normally one to smile, Linda does have another side and some of her tears are displayed on the following pages.

TO THE AUTHORITARIANS

If we're going to play
   cops and robbers
don't expect me to
   help carry your keys.

If you place a label
   over my personality
don't expect me to
   treat you as an individual.

If you really want me
to succeed in this world,
don't keep telling me,
   through your words and deeds,
that I've already failed.

There is more to life
than making imprint
through carbon copy.

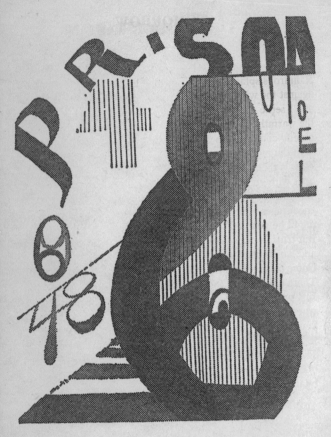

48 to 69: Prison Music by Othello Noel

TOMORROW

Raindrops splash softly
against the windowpane
and I settle deeper into
the warmth; beside you,
quietly content, at peace
with the night.
Now is the time for talk,
be it with god or man.
The melody trickling over Autumn leaves
encourages honesty that, at another time,
might be guarded too heavily for truth.
But trust does not come easily,
and words often not at all.
Come close to me; be patient.
There are things I want to tell you.
Just promise me that
when the rain goes
you will send my words
to keep it company.
The past will never change,
but it's possible to ruin the present
by thinking too much about the future.

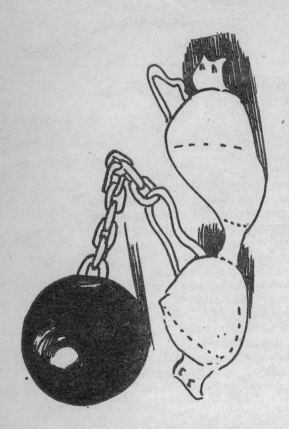

Ball-broken by Othello Noel

REFLECTING

There is a poster clinging
to my white stone wall;
a paper mirage.
The broken-post fence and dusty leaves
prod memories of country roads long past,
quiet times of shaded glens,
afternoons when we were alone together.
I've known country roads before,
but it's been months
and nothing much is left,
other than a touch of sun and closeness,
reflecting on the summer of country roads,
wanting you.

ESCAPE

At night sometimes
I can lose myself
between the pages
of a book.

I forget the facts
of living in a prison:
   showers never clean,
   food with no taste,
   living with strangers.

Living with strangers.

But the book always ends
and that end is the beginning
of my return to the facts
of living in a prison:
   showers never clean,
   food with no taste,
   living with strangers.

Living with . . .

I don't read as much as I used to.
Coming back, sometimes,
is worse than never leaving.

In mate by A.O.A.

SO AS NOT TO FORGET

Touch me with your eyes.
Words are cheap and the things
we have to say lie heavy in the air.

Touch me with your smile.
It warms the open spaces left vacant
by those who cannot, or will not, see.

Touch me with your heart.
Because at this time, in this place,
I need softness, and someone to trust.

Talk to me of trees and streams
and things out of doors.
I know of floors and walls
and artificial lights.

Remind me of the ocean,
of the salt and spray
and smell of seawater
cascading over jagged rocks.

Tell me of early-morning skies,
of clouds whipped into
mare's tails by the
master sculptor, Wind.

Don't let me forget these things,
of life and living.
Your light chases dark shadows
from a lonely heart.

There is a noise here
that some call music.
It has no rhythm
and is not music to me.

Music is love,
ocean waves caressing shore,
tenor sax, sparkling snow,
holding hands in the rain.

Music is life,
young grass thrusting upward,
children laughing, playing.
Sunshine in my eyes.

I miss that music.
You bring it in with you,
but it doesn't like to stay
once you've gone.

Could you come more often?

THE GAME

How did I come to be here
    you ask?
At a time long past
    when I knew no better
    I was given directions
    how to get
    from one place to another
    a better place.
But I ended up
    here instead.
Pawn to King's three.

Why don't I leave?
Well
    you see
    I can't
    the game isn't over yet
    the pawn is still on the board
    being sacrificed
    to protect the King.
Nothing personal
    a matter of
    self-preservation
    I guess.

Please get me out
   if you can find me
   before the game is over.
If not
   I may soon concede.

THE WITHERED

People here?
People here
resemble trees that
have stopped growing.
Mostly they
look the same.
Some have
lost leaves but
they will come back if
the tree reaches sunlight.
Some have
broken branches, no
amount of sun will
ever heal them completely.

BOB CHINN—

Rahway State Prison, New Jersey

Bob Chinn is one of those quiet individuals who walks softly and carries a big stick. Rarely will you see or hear this man as he goes about handling his 25-year bid, but when he does evidence himself, it is always with an impact that stuns.

SARFARI

I found a nice room on Sterling Street. The room was two short blocks from a drug scene. Methodically, my actions were aimed at one thing—getting high!

About a week later, a very noticeable roomer approached me, introduced himself as my down-the-hall neighbor and asked if I knew how to play pinochle. I replied yes and told him that I was the best in the world. He smiled, held out his hand and said, "Buster." I took his hand. "Bob—glad to meet you."

We went into the kitchen. Buster introduced me to his wife, Chip. I said "noticeable roomer" because Buster was impossible not to notice: blue-black, 6-4, about 250 lbs. It would take more than two bullets to stop him.

"Got time for a few games?" Buster asked hopefully.

I rubbed my hands together. "Yeah."

"Chip, he said that he's the best in the whole world."

Chip looked at me, then at Buster. "You used to say that, too."

We got down to business.

That night I learned two things about Buster and Chip: they weren't too long from the South, and they played a damned good game of pinochle.

Buster came to Newark from Alabama, found a job with a meat packing company, saved some money, went back to Alabama, got married and returned to Newark with his bride. Aside from his no nonsense demeanor, he was pleasant, likable and loyal. I liked him.

Chip was brown-skinned, 5-6, 110 lbs., comely, devoted, and like Buster, not too quick to make friends. She worked part time (day domestic). She was a born homemaker. Chip had a warm engaging smile. A smile that I wouldn't mind coming home to.

Through pinochle, Buster, Chip and I cultivated a warm, unpretentious friendship with family overtones. When Chip's mother died, they went South to bury Mama. Buster entrusted me with their household paraphernalia. When they returned, exhausted, at eleven o'clock in the morning, I persuaded them, without objections, to take a nap in my bed before rearranging their room.

Buster and Chip didn't know anything about drugs, and they never pressed me for any personal information. I felt a twinge of loneliness when Buster told me they were moving into the projects on the first of the coming month.

Someone tapped on my door. "Who?"

"Chip," came the reply.

Before I could throw the sheet back to get up, the door opened. Chip stepped in, closed the door, walked over and sat meekly on the side of my bed.

"Good mornin', Chip."

She managed a weak smile. "Something ain't right down there."

I waited a few moments for clarification. "What are you talkin' about?"

"I itch something awful!"

"Where?"

"Down there."

She avoided my eyes. "I . . . washed . . . and as soon as I finished, I scratched til I got sore! I got a mirror and looked. I don't know . . . I couldn't see anything. But I know there's something down there that ain't got no business down there!"

"You think you've got the crabs?"

"Uh huh. What do you think?"

"I don't know, Chip. But if you think you've got them, got to the drug store and ask for something to clear it up."

"Huh? I couldn't do that! I'd die of embarrassment."

"Well get someone . . . you want me to get you something?"

She nodded yes.

"Did you tell Buster?"

"No."

"Why?"

I sensed that she didn't want to talk about it. As she opened the door to leave, she turned and said, "I-don't know, Bob. I—"

The next morning in the kitchen, I gave Chip the eye telling her that I had something for her. A few minutes later, she was sitting on my bed with a tube of ointment in her hands.

"Bob, I'm scared!"

"Come on now, that stuff ain't—"

"I don't mean that. Suppose . . . I think maybe Buster has caught 'em from me."

"Do you have any idea when you caught them?"

"I-don't know . . . about two weeks ago."

"When you went South to bury your mother?"

"I think so . . . yes."

"About how many times have you and Buster had intercourse since you've been back?"

"Buster is too big for me . . . we don't want children yet."

"Then, how do you figure he caught them?"

"We—"

"How many times have you done whatever you do?"

"Two times."

"Two times? Are you sure? Well, the way I see it, you started itchin' about five or six days ago. Right?"

"Uh huh."

"Then, you ain't got nothing to worry about. He ain't infected. Now read the directions on the tube. After you do what the directions say, put on a sanitary napkin so you don't have to worry about Buster botherin' you for the next three days. Then you're back in business. Okay?"

Three days later, after Buster went to work at six o'clock in the morning, Chip tap-tap-tapped me awake. I staggered to the door, clicked the latch off, stumbled to the bed and got back in. "Everything workin' out okay?" I yawned.

"I don't think so."

I lit a cigarette and cursed myself out for getting involved.

Chip sat on the side of the bed and started wringing her hands. "I think I still got 'em and my period started this mornin'."

"Did you get a mirror and look?"

"Yes, but I don't know what to look for."

"Chip, you're impossible. What are you goin' to do now? All you had to do was to tell Buster that you caught them in a train or bus station toilet, and you can still tell him that." I was beginning to loose my patience.

Chip shook her head from side to side; she was on the verge of tears. "Buster believes that there's only one way that you can catch the crabs."

"Then you've got to swallow your modesty, go to a doctor, let him shave you clean and put something on to kill the eggs that are buried in the skin. In fact, you can do it yourself."

"Buster would notice me not havin' any hair."

"Chip, shave all but a little patch of hair on top, part the patch into rows and look for hairs with eggs on them. When you find one, pull out the hair with tweezers."

Chip looked down at her feet. "Bob, would you help me, please?"

"Chip, you're insane!" I went into the bathroom and took a fix.

While telling myself over and over, "Chinn, it ain't none of your business!" I put on a stocking cap, old shirt and pants. I stripped the bed, placed newspapers over the mattress and floor and spread a sheet over the newspapers and mattress. Then I got a basin of hot water, the soap and a razor. I told Chip to tie her hair up, take off her slip and to put on a tight-fitting blouse or sweater. I tied a string around a wad of cotton; she inserted it into her vagina.

I showed her the position. She took off her skirt and got on her hands and knees with her feet hanging over the edge of the bed. The position elevated her buttocks so I could shave the hair around her anus.

Aware of the fact that a small nick could present a big problem, I lathered and clean shaved all the hair in and around her anal area very carefully. As I applied a film of ointment, I said jokingly, "Chip, if it starts feelin' hot back here, tell me so I can blow on it."

She replied jokingly, "It does burn a little."

"Yeah? Stay just the way you are. I'll call Buster and tell him your butt is on fire and for him to come home and blow out the flames."

Much relieved, now that half of the "safari" was over, I told her to sit on the side of the bed and lie back. I spread and propped both her legs on chairs, lathered and shaved all but a little patch of hair on top. In spite of my being high, her womanhood got through to me. Reluctantly, so I could see better, I got down on my knees. With tweezers, I searched for crabs and eggs. Every now and then, the picture of an irate Buster would shoot through my mind; I paused, shook my head and looked over at the feeble latch on the door! After I was satisfied the area was clear, I applied the ointment.

Silently, we put my room back in order. She reached for the doorknob to leave.

"Chip, suppose while you were lyin' there, I took the advantage of you. What would you have done?"

She thought about it, smiled and shrugged her shoulders. "I don't know. Bob, right after Buster went North, Mama got sick. I started goin' out with a man from Mobile; he helped us out a lot. When Buster found a job, he sent me money; he came back, we got married and left. When we went back to bury Mama, I saw and talked with the man I'd taken up with while Buster was away. He was very bitter and said that I had misled and used him. I thanked him for helpin' me and my family, but he said that that wasn't enough. He wanted me to sleep with him just one time. I had used him. So I went to bed with him. You know the rest of the story. Bob, thanks!"

*BLESHIN'!**

Black woman, blesh with me.
Don't submit, receive and thrill
only to my mindless appendage.
There is more, much more!

Black woman, take what is yours.
Thrust your vibrant soul against the
white hymen blockin' my soul's womb.
I've been had, but I want to be raped by you!

Black woman, handle me.
Split my beauhead, probe deeply and
demand an audience with your natural mate.
When I see you, I'll know me!

Black woman, I want to blesh with you.
Plunge vigorously into my dejected soul, then
kindle and germinate my awareness of you!
Now hush, let's blesh . . .

*Blesh: to copulate spiritually, mentally
and physically simultaneously.

ZE

Demure Ze!
Very comely she be.
Submerged in the warmth
  of her infectious smile,
I simmered!
Her jacks-hopscotch-ropejumpin' days
  whizzed by.
"It won't be long!" I sighed.
Things sprouted and bloomed.
Bayin' beaux fussed and fumed.
To us, it seemed all too soon;
"Haste," we cried,
  "leads to heartbreak and doom!"
We were wrong.
They composed a beautiful song,
  then two,
  then three—
"Lighten up, Ze!"
Our affair lives within/without cease.
You see, she's my niece . . . .

THE UNMOLESTED ALARM CLOCK

Awed from the pleasure of giving, engulfed by total darkness, two nude lovers gave of themselves after stealing behind a partition. Each was aware only of the other and their need to satisfy the needs of each other. This was a joyous occasion—their reality, their moment of truth. There were so many pleasurable things to do, and each conjured in the other indescribable pleasures that surged delightfully through their hungry bodies, causing them to cry and moan. Possessed, they clamped their mouths together and savored. In reverie, they sighed and cooed to each other's caresses. Uninhibited, they conversed with their bodies. Each rejuvenated by basking in the other's fallout. Their's was total. Their's was urgent. Their's was now! "I love you" was expressed in many modes, rendering the recipient exhausted and limp. They were caught in the clutches of a sadistic rapture! Time and time again, they soared through heat waves of torrid bliss. The black surrendered her cherished soul, the white vowed lifelong obedience. Ascending with anticipation, an ultra apex would soon be theirs—

"All right, you two, the party's over!"

They reacted to the statement as though they had been doused with ice water. Blinded by the sudden light, they clung fearfully to each other!

"I knew you two sluts had the hots for each other. Break it up before I break you up!"

Bloodcurdling rage swept through the convicts like wildfire!! They attacked the stick-wielding matron.

115

Mary Potter was awake long before the alarm clock rang. When it rang, she let it ring itself out. Mary didn't cut it off because she couldn't cut it off. Nor could she visualize the two young inmates who had escaped five years ago, leaving her maimed for life!

Mary had watched hotly as the girls made love. Their joy had gratified her. She had fingered herself lustily. The stark realization of what she was had shamed her. Fearing a resurgence, she had halted the girls before their fulfillment was complete.

Mary's guilt was great: less than an hour after their escape, arm in arm, the escapees hurled their vibrant young bodies from a high-rise apartment building! Mary's punishment was great, also: she was a blind voyeur . . . .

PUBESCENCE!

I ran and hid! What will she do? Did I hurt her? She was whimpering when I left. Will she have me put away? Was she asleep and think that it was only a dream? Did she call me? What happened? I walked into her room and there she was, lying there naked! I called her; she didn't respond. I tipped over, turned the light out and thought about pulling the sheet up over her—that's when it happened! Her nakedness drew me like a magnet! She's the first women I ever saw completely nude! Awed, I caressed, kissed and licked her bothersome feet and brushed my closed lips over the fine hairs on her strong legs. Her thighs felt cool to my nestling cheeks. I parted her legs and kneed catlike between them. Little by little, my fingers traced her waist and hips. Like a butterfly, I snuggled my face to her crotch. My hands inched up to cover her breast. Gently, I blew hot breath against her private and pried its lips open with the tip of my tongue. She stirred! I withdrew my tongue and hovered motionlessly! She eased one leg back, then the other. Like a flower, her private parted. Its fragrance was heady! She relaxed. Lightly, I cupped my mouth over her opening. Her nipples felt like dagger-points against the palms of my hands. I could feel her pulse beating strongly against my top lip. My tongue explored the length and width of her outer opening. I lingered on a spot that felt like a small tit. I ran my tongue across it again and again. The tit became erect like my penis. She spread her legs further apart. An urgency seemed to come over her. She seized

117

my head with both hands! I began to feel her urgency in my swollen private! She sighed and rubbed my head. Suddenly, I was overcome by an impulse to enter her opening! I freed my head. Fretfully, she pawed the air as her crotch pursued my lips. I pulled my pajamas down, threw myself upon her and pentrated the depth of her private! She gasped! In a frenzy, I thrust myself into her time after time! Hungrily, my mouth found and sucked her breast! Roughly, with one hand, I cupped and kneaded her buttocks; my other hand wrung her hair! Slowly, her protesting sobs and feeble attempts to dislodge me were replaced by an inner turmoil that spread like wildfire through her private into mine! I clutched her to me, shuddered and savored!! The stark realization of what I had done lifted me off grandma's prostrated body! I ran and hid!

"Thomas!"

Oh, my God—grandma!?

"Thomas? I know you hear me. Where are you?"

I can't let her find me. Not after what I just did! I can't face grandma! If I can ease the window open without her hearing me, I'll—

"Thomas," she said softly, "I know you're in there. c'mon out. Grandma wanta talk to you."

Shamefaced, I shuffled out!

Grandma was wearing my momma's housecoat. My momma left us ten years ago when I was four years old. I never met my father. Grandma said that we got some relatives up North; we never hear from them.

"Thomas?" she said as she uncrossed her arms and held them open for me to enter. "Thomas, you're a young man now; a good young man. I should've sold this old house and took you up North. I been puttin' it off hopin' that your momma would come home. Don't feel bad; grandma still loves you. Boy, your grandma ain't had a man since your grandpa passed, sixteen years ago. It wasn't all your fault . . . I think I set it up to happen. Thanks, Thomas. But boy, mind! After you make love to a woman, don't get up and run! Kiss her, Thomas, kiss her . . ."

WITH THIS HAND

The hum of the wing's blower . . .
As was yesterday and the yesterdays before that—
the morn of another long, dull day!
My manhood is awake, also. Ah, it feels delicious!
How many times have I awakened with this urge—
surgin' . . . pleadin' that I heed my need to seed?
How many times have I yielded?
Yielded to seed a woman . . . or a fat-butt boy?
Nay—only my hand . . . a rough hand . . . a sure
hand . . .
a hand that synchronizes its grip and syncopation
to stimulate a rollickin', yawnin' vagina!
A vagina that I conjured from the past—
the image of a good piece of ass with a mass
that did last through these long, lean years!
A tired hand . . . a good hand!
The dusky image becomes vivid: her rampant afro, her
half-closed eyelids, her flarin' nostrils, her parted
lips, her sighs, her take-me-you're-mine expression,
her noble breasts, her shallow navel, her fragrant
chasm—scorchin', soggy, firm, grapplin', poppin',
gyratin' . . . I thrust counter to my hand!
The urge becomes a demand!
No—not yet! Not yet! She wants to ride the greasy pole!
She's above me; her breasts are danglin' before my eyes!
Slowly her snatch devours its catch . . . our hairs mesh!
I squeeze her breasts together and knead both nipples

119

with my tongue . . . the juice from my rigid member
annoints my ravishin' fist . . . that glorious spread suckin'
me deeper,
deeper, deeper, back whence I came to come again . . . to
cum,
to cum! Cum! CuM! CUM!
The hum of the wing's blower . . .

HUH?

Love?
Is love beautiful, pleasurable & healthy?
Or is it ugly, painful & harmful?
Why are we discouraged from makin' love?
Are lovers a threat to our society?
You can get busted for makin' love!
If the "man" catches Jill filled with Jack in the sack,
he can arrest the act & get them a love-makin' rap!
What's wrong with makin' love?
You cãn get committed to a hosipital for lovin' a human
    being!
If two Jills get caught feastin' on each other's hills,
our anti-love establishment will prescribe
banishment & guilt pills!
Who are lovers harmin' when they make love?
You can get a long, jail sentence for receivin' or givin' joy!
If two Jacks get caught jackin' each other's jacks,
our confused & perverse morality will cut
them apart with the hate and warmonger's axe!
When will we cease apin' the meddlesome dove and
not attack lovers for makin' love?

HATTIE

Hattie, about 24, was a retired prostitute. When her white, lesbian pimp became a dealer and took her off the streets, Hattie became her former pimp's go-between and bag-woman. When we met (1961), she was functioning in the latter capacity. Shortly afterwards, I met her "man," Sammie.

Sammie, about 35, had been on the scene (Lenox Avenue, between 117th and 118th Streets) about ten years and Hattie was her woman. Other than that, Sammie was a mystery. No one on the scene knew, or would admit knowing, her real name, where she hailed from, where she (they) really lived or if she was "sho'nuff" white.

Although Sammie and Hattie were on the scene just about everyday, Sammie didn't "deal" consistently. Every now and then she would come out with a damned good bag. No one could predict just when Sammie would be doing something. And if she was doing something, you had to cop through Hattie. Sammie let Hattie do all the selling. They were not junkies.

Hattie and I had seen each other a number of times, but she didn't approach me until after she saw a well-known controller instruct one of his pushers to give me two bags to sample. As was the custom at that time, when a new batch was coming out, the controllers of the new batch would pass out samples to old junkies and cop men. After that, when Sammie was doing, Hattie would give me a few bags to sample, and I'd tell her what I thought about Sammie's stuff in relation to other stuff that was being sold on the

122

street at that time. We became fairly good friends. I was never sick when Sammie was doing.

Sammie, Hattie and I became very good friends when Sammie became ill. I had seen Hattie a few times, but I didn't recall seeing Sammie with her. When I inquired where and how was Sammie, Hattie said that Sammie was laying up because she wasn't feeling too well. One afternoon, after asking Hattie how Sammie was doing, Hattie asked me to meet her that night at 7:30 at the restaurant on the corner of Lenox Avenue and 117th Street.

That night, when I got to the restaurant, Hattie was sitting at the counter, talking to a waitress. When I entered, she left the counter and sat at a table that was next to a telephone booth. I joined her. She handed me the menu.

"Hungry? Order something."

I ordered something.

"Sammie is in the hospital. She suppose to call me here at 8 o'clock, and she wanta talk to you. I told her that you were lookin' out for me. She said that you were good people."

"Anything serious?"

"Yeah. She gotta have an operation."

"Do you know why she wants to talk to me?"

"I think I do, but I'm not sure. So I think I should wait and let her tell you. Do you ever think about goin' back to Jersey?"

"Jersey?"

"Ray calls you his homie; he's from Jersey."

"Are you a native New Yorker?"

"You're a musician. I can tell by that light spot on your top lip. Right?"

The telephone rang. Hattie answered the phone. It was Sammie; Hattie closed the door. About two minutes later, she opened the door, motioned for me to come there and handed me the phone.

"Sammie?"

"Yeah, Bob. How're you doing?"

"Oh, I'm makin' it. How're you comin' along?"

"They wanta operate. Hattie told me you're looking out for her, thanks. Bob, I've got a job for you if you think you can handle it. I'm going to be laid up for a while, but I've got to make an important move, now. The only person I can trust to make the move is Hattie. I can't let her make the move without some protection. That's the job, protecting Hattie while she's taking care of business. Listen, I don't expect any trouble, but I can't let her do it alone. It should take about an hour. Now, if you give me your word to stick with her while she's making the move, I'll tell her to give you a gun, and when the job is finished, to pay you a hundred dollars. I can't tell you what the move is until you tell me whether you can handle it."

"If you want me to off or take off somebody, no good. Anything else, I can handle it."

"Okay, dig. I've got a batch of stuff I cut with bonito and quinine. If I let the stuff lay, it will lose its strength. So I'm going to sell the whole batch. Hattie is going to rent a room in a hotel. Then she'll call the people and tell them when and where to pick up the stuff. When they come, Hattie will count the money, and they can test the stuff if they want to. Keep them covered, and don't let them leave the room until Hattie has counted the money. After the sale is over, stay with her until she's in a cab.

"Bob, listen—Hattie isn't a stupid bitch. She knows how to set it up, and she can spot bad money a mile away. If she says 'no deal,' don't take any chances, pull your piece and get them out of the room, fast! Hattie knows what to do if that should happen. Remember, you can rely on her judgment. Do you have any questions?"

"No."

"Okay. Put Hattie back on."

Hattie stepped out of the booth. As she sat, I noticed a faraway look in her eyes. She observed: "You were hungry."

"Yeah. Well, boss, when are you goin' to set it up?"

"It's all set up. Tonight."

"Tonight?"

"Uh huh. I bought you some clothes. All you have to do is—"

"Get a haircut, shave and take a bath. I can do the last two, but I don't think we can find a barber shop open at this hour."

Hattie smiled. "I can trim hair, too."

"I've got a feelin' that you've got everything all figured to the last detail. So, lead the way, boss. Oh, I almost forgot. I have to pick up my works."

"Where we're goin', there's stuff and two brand-new sets of works. How's that for a starter?"

"Mmmm, you're valuable. It's a wonder Sammie trusts me with you."

"Sammie knows that junkies don't screw."

She paid for my something. We left the restaurant, hailed a cab, and after she gave the cabby our destination, we sped to my badly-needed bath.

Hattie took me to a furnished room that was on the third floor of a rooming house on 137th Street, between 7th and 8th Avenues. The room belonged to a man. "Do you wanta trim my hair first?"

"Are you kiddin'?"

"Do I smell that bad?"

"Yeah."

"Aren't you afraid that you'll offend me?"

"Tell the truth, who's offendin' who?"

I had never thought of myself as being superior or inferior to women, but Hattie made me feel inferior . . . and uncouth.

I shaved, bathed, took a fix, put on my strange new outfit, that fit like a glove, then presented myself for inspection.

"Pull that chair under the light so I can do something about your hair."

As she snipped away, she told me the set up: "When we leave, take those three pieces of luggage. We'll catch a cab to the Theresa Hotel. I've made reservations for a Mr. and Mrs. Robert Robinson, Harrisburg, Pa. After we're in the room about 15 minutes, I'll make the call. You know what to do after that?"

I nodded my head.

"Hold still. By the way, there ain't no stuff in the luggage."

"Okay. Shake the sheet out in the hall. I'll clean this up."

When I stepped back into the room, she handed me a loaded Police .38 special in a belt-clip holster. I examined the gun, put it back in the holster, clipped it to my belt, then put on my suit jacket.

"Turn around so I can look at you. Uh huh. If I was workin' the streets, I wouldn't trick with you. You look like a cop."

"Hattie, that's the second nice thing you've said to me to-night."

"What was the first?"

"Order something."

The money was right (about $3000). Hattie had missed her calling, she should have been a bank cashier. It still wasn't too late. She finished counting before the two white guys, who looked like they were from the Village, finished testing the stuff. When they finished, they put the stuff in a bowling bag and left. There was no conversation. Then, we made our surprise getaway.

As soon as the door closed, she pantomimed for me to listen at the door. She pulled her flair skirt and half slip down, put the money in a money belt that was around her waist, pulled her skirt and slip back up, coolly opened her handbag, pulled out an unsexy, nickel-plated revolver, walked over to me, unbuttoned my jacket and took my (her) gun. "Did you hear them get on the elevator?"

"Yeah."

"Forget the luggage. We're leavin' through the fire exit. You first, now!"

When we got to the street, she pointed to a powder-blue, late-model Chevy. She unlocked the door, got behind the wheel, reached over and unlocked the door for me. I got in. She cranked up, drove around the block and parked near the 25th Precinct.

"Yeah, I know: you can drive, too." The car was a rental.

"Here's the hundred dollars Sammie promised you. Sorry about the gun, but Sammie needs this money. Now, while you're all cleaned up, I want you to do me a favor. Tomorrow at one o'clock, I want you to go with me to visit Sammie. I'll give you a half-a-load."

"No good. I dig Sammie. You don't have to pay me. Just tell me where to meet you."

"Thanks. I was wrong and Sammie was right about you. She said that you wouldn't try anything. I was apprehensive because when a man catch a woman in a compromisin' position, he usually socks it to her. You know what I mean."

"Yeah. If it'll make you feel any better, if I were together, you would have had a little trouble out of me. You see, I've never wrestled with a woman who weighed over 150 pounds."

She gave me a broad smile. "See you tomorrow at one o'clock on the corner of 5th Avenue and 116th Street."

The next day, when Hattie and I left the hospital, I knew something that no one on the scene knew. I had met Sammie's mother who looked young enough to be Sammie's sister, her uncle (father's brother), and her bony, uncute, teen-age cousin. Sammie was "sho'nuff" white. . . .

NORMAN PORTER—

State Correctional Institution, Norfolk, Massachusets

Norman Porter could easily have taken another course and ended up a governor or, at the very least, in the U.S. Senate. However, the winds of influence landed him in a prison, but that didn't stop him from hustling for the things he believed in. Yet those accomplishments would require more print than GONE WITH THE WIND, so for the moment we will have to content ourselves with these written portraits he has submitted.

I CREEP ALONG TO GETTING OLD

I creep along to getting old
some thinning thoughts here
some bald passions there.

Why was it so important
   when I was nine to be nineteen?

And now that I'm way past nineteen
   why is it so important to be nineteen again?

I know more now than I did then
   but I knew even more at nine.

I profess no rush to grow old
no desire to tinker
   like old men always have
   with widowed old ladies down the street
   where a peek of bloomers
   stirs the energy to recall a whole life.

This thought just seems to end . . .

Why is it so important to be nineteen again?

The tree has roots by Patricia Krenwinkle

PRISON

Everybody expects a prison to be mean
everybody wants a prison to be mean
to be the incarnate embodiment
of the very same evil
they were designed to contain
cold, sterile lock-aways
built and maintained
for the protection
   of good
   of justice
   of mother
hidden deep in the bowels
of the community
acting like lonely old crones
taking daily physics
to rid their tired bodies
of imagined lodged filth
and the reacting fearful community
dispenses cascading waves
of purges
through social strata
depressing the imagined lodged criminal
in the evacuation that flows
through justice colon
the half-digested the half formed
pass their usefulness expended
destined for the toilet bowl named jail
everybody expects a prison to be mean
everybody wants a prison to be mean
and they are.

LOCKED IN: PART ONE

And at the hour after 9:00 post meridiem
my cell door swings shut like the cover of a coffin
and the polished mahogany bars thud
against the silk covered pine frame
and the locking bolt is struck
like the hot lead slug of a .357 magnum
and I am alone.

And at the hour after 10:00 post meridiem
my life-sustaining electric light clips off
and the very light I need turns black
against the flashing brilliance of a coho salmon
at the end of Marlon Brando's line
and flopping on the shore of my bed
I die.

LOCKED IN: PART TWO

And at the hour of 6:30 ante meridiem
my cell door explodes with the scroonch of an axed willow
and the rush of uncontained oxygen pours in
and lifts me from under the covers
and I know another day is here
and in the stingy sweat to get the last pound
I am punished.

And at these hours between 6:30 ante and 11:00 post
  meridiem
my life swirls in constant fantasy
at the illusion of the light at the end of the tunnel
like some insane mental cripple
confined to a sick hospital like he were Jesus
and it appears we walk the same way to heaven
but I am alone.

SOMEWHERE ELSE

In my barred ringed room
I often dream of being somewhere else
where I could shed this shadow
I lean upon and act myself
without benefit of pretense
cowed under by degrees
to the man's psycho-whip
as I keep myself in good standing
even though sold out
what a need to escape all that
and take myself to the woods
on leaves of mental image
like someone feigning Napoleon
and trip across the fields
barefoot in flight on hoarfrost
gone quick in the morning light
like my thoughts
gone quick in hearing
the screw's whistle
up in evaporation
not at all like
the solid state
of my barred ringed room.

FUNERAL

I went to a funeral today
roses smelled my nose
half-opened lid cover
exposed my thoughts
for others to mourn
I celebrated
death and rebirth
worm to cocoon
to spirit
floating free
mourners marched by
1776 exploded
brass shells expended
handkerchiefs dampened
I celebrated
my own death
while others mourned
my passing
roses smelled my nose
I went to a funeral today.

GETTING UP

Sitting here in solitude
on the rock hard bunk
of my prison cell
I feel constricted
and powerless
as if the loneliness
robbed me of my strength
to face the day
and see it through
with eyes gone crimson
like the iron bars.

I cross my legs
I uncross my legs
nothing seems right
in belonging here
in this prison world
of ritualized procedure
written down
in thousand copies
and memorized by heart
to start and stop
by whistles, bells and gongs.

I write these words
out of sheer desperation
to fill the void

138

that echoes so empty
inside of me
pounding my life forces
to crippled functions
that grow tired and weary
just to get up in the morning
and I have to gasp
and struggle
to avoid suffocating.

I CAME TO WRITE A POEM

I came to write a poem
and found only words
cluttering my brain.

In some speck of eternity
I suppose these words would be enough
for anyone else to use for a poem.

But for me, down where I write
in the stocking of my mind,
I suspect these words will fail me.

Othello Noel

YESTERDAY I DID THE SAME THING

Yesterday I did the same thing
I did for 4000 days.
I spent my time doing time
in the neglected hallways
of my master's house.
Cobweb's spin spiders in my head:
rabbits run wildly domesticated
and breed no youngin':
elephant tusks made of copper,
someone once rigged a still
and made gallons and gallons of green beef stew
and fed it to us for supper:
striped tigers assault non-striped tigers
—no violence here—
they have no teeth and only gum each other
in the nooks and crannies of the square concrete building;
little old ladies carry machine guns
spitting out regulations and rules killing everyone
with wad after wad of emaciated tampoons:
the shadow knows what evil lurks
in the key tumblers that lock men's eyelashes
and breathes down his neck
his own foul breath
4000 days.

WIFFED PUFFS OF HAZE

Wiffed puffs of haze
pelt my forehead
dripping rivulets
of broken mist
into the corners
of my eyes
and I can see
why I write poems
like this.
What other way
to say
that I felt
for an instant
for a brief instant
what that haze was.
And to tell you
with words that recall
—not words that were there—
a poem is where I've been.
To you it might be
a wiffed puff of haze
then you and I can both say
we saw what was worth a poem, once
and now we're trying to remember.

HENRY LUCAS—

Florida State Prison, Starke, Florida

Henry Lucas, writing under the pseudonym *eusi profile*, is an angry black man who for years has been fruitlessly hollering at the walls. He sent his writings to me handwritten on some of the raggediest paper in existence, explaining to me that the Florida Prison System doesn't allow its inmates to own their own typewriters. In most cases, men are forced to compile and present handwritten briefs to the Court of Appeals, so this makes it a double crime, because Henry Lucas, or *eusi profile*, is a writer and a damn good one! His contributions to PROSE AND CONS were penned in the hole with a bare floor as a table.

dehumanization

. . . for brothers in prison . . .
. . . who fear liberation . . .

BUZZZZ/ah mindshatterin electrical command blares/
    meanin . . .
it's 6 o'clock in de mornin/time to get up/but . . .
it's gotta be earlier than 6 o'clock in de mornin/cause . . .
de sun hasn't even showed on de scene/yet . . .
already ya dehumanized feet done hit de concrete floor of
    ya cell/movin . . .
without waitin for a command from ya brain
ah brain dat has long ago ceased to function
beyond de monotonous prison schedule
ya dehumanized hands reach for ya face cloth
SPLASH-SPLASH/WATER-WATER/BRUSH-
    BRUSH/TEETH-TEETH/GURGLE-GURGLE
CLANG/BANG/POP/NOISE-NOISE
ya cell door is unlocked/permittin access to de larger cell
COMB-COMB/PICK-PICK/ya micro-afro
dat de nicenasty prison administration permits ya to sport
said ya might hide ah pistol in ah large afro/HOW RIDIC-
    ULOUS
said ya might hide ah pistol in ah large afro . . .
same O/jive lie dat they used to cover up/their . . .
coldblooded murder of a brother
white folks are ah most bitch with their halfslick shit
(de suckers just be mad cause handsome black you

147

don't wanna look like ugly white them no more)

betcha they wouldn't produce no static if ya fried half ya
    brains out

so dat ya boss/curly hair could strangely resemble broom
    straws

CHOW TIME/PAIR IT UP

ya dehumanized feet shuffle outta de door

pairin-up with another dehumanized body

mechanically streakin to de MESS hall to feed ya face

& breakfast be like all de other tasteless/mouthdryin/sloppy
    meals

ya eat fast/shovin de food to de back of ya mouth

tryin hard not to pollute ya tongue with it

ya gobble de slop up swiftly for another reason too/cause . . .

ya had to learn thru unceartin Xperiences

dat ah prisoner doesn't pick thru de food

if he Xpects to keep his appetite

he eats FAST-FAST/blottin outta his mind

de rat parts/bugs/mop strings & other shocks

dat frequently pop-up in de food

even tho they are never printed on de menu

paired-up/dehumanized feet shuffle back to ya cell

make up bunk/sweepup floor/mopup floor/pull ya cell to-
    gether

BUZZZZ/dat deafenin electrical command blares again

succeeded by ah tobacco chewer's voice/screechin . . .

COUNT TIME COUNT TIME/ALL INMATES LOCK
    YER CELL DOOR & GET ON THE DOOR FOR
    COUNT TIME . . .

ALL WING OFFICERS GIVE ME A COUNT (instant
    repeat) COUNT TIME COUNT TIME/ALL INMATES
LOCK YER CELL DOOR & GET ON THE DOOR FOR
    COUNT TIME . . . ALL WING OFFICERS GIVE
    ME A COUNT

ya heard somebody down the line/scream . . .

YOU FUGGIN PRICK GO HOME & COUNT YOUR
    GRANNY'S FLOUR SACK DRAWERS

but already ya dehumanized self/done followed instructions
    to ah TEE

after de buzzards pass by & count ya/ya catch up ya bunk

snatchup a novel & proceed to trip to ah wonderful world
    of fantasy

cause ya be knowin it's gonna take

for what seems like hours for them to count

de buzzards mustta sidestepped countin lessons

durin their (if ever for them there were) school days

after what seemed like ah mighty heappa forever

& ah whole buncha days

BUZZZZ/dat deafin electrical command blares again

& ah tobacco chewer's voice/proclaims . . .

THE COUNT IS CLEAR THE COUNT IS CLEAR

CLANG/BANG/POP/NOISE-NOISE

cell doors fly open/like de restta de prisoners

ya dash into de larger cell

(so relieved dat de electrical master hadn't again com-
    manded/RECOUNT-RECOUNT)

prisoners assimilate here & there signifyin/shootin de bull

or playin whatever institutionalized game

dat was their favorite pass de time away

down de line from where you stood assimilated/playin ya
    pass de time away

ya saw ah buzzard & a brother arguin bout somethin

ya heard de brother/shoutin . . .

DAT HE WAS AH HUMAN BEIN NOT SOME DEHU-
    MANIZED THING

& IF DE BUZZARD WANTED RESPECT FROM HIM

HE HAD BETTA LEARN HOW TO GIVE RESPECT
    TO HIM

ya saw de redfaced buzzard reachin for ah disciplinary
    report/but . . .

ya refocused ya attention to doin ya thing

dismissin de incident as contrary to institutional life

BUZZZZ/dat deafenin electrical command blares again

& de same-O tobacco chewer's voice/screeches . . .

WORK SQUADS-WORK SQUADS/ALL WING OFFI-
   CERS SEND UP YER WORK SQUADS
automatically ya dehumanized feet shuffle toward de door
to wait for de buzzards to screech ya squad
(ya squad is screeched)
ya shuffle out de door/gazin at de other prisoners paired-up
& bein herded like cows to their work assignments
while de prison guards (like de buzzards dat they are)
watch de paired-up cows
ready to swoop down on de first one
dat stumbles & falls outta line
with ah talon-full of disciplinary reports
& ah beak-full of foul language
de human dat is still left in ya rallies (for ah second)
& ya think . . . YA NOT AH THING/YA NOT AH COM-
   PUTERIZED
INSTITUTIONALIZED NUMERALIZED DEHUMAN-
   IZED THING
YA MORE THAN AH NUMBER STAMPED ON A MUG
   SHOT
YA HUMAN DAMMIT YA HUMAN/DE BROTHER
   WAS RIGHT . . .
(another second) de human dat was still left in ya
   vanishes . . .
forever buried in ah filin cabinet dat must not be used
if ever ya gonna get rehabilitated
ya herd began to cautiously shuffle pass de lurkin buzzards
ah bell tinkles round ya neck & with ah low
   MOOOO/YOU . . .
ya shuffle in time to de rhythm of ya herd
cause ya done come ah perfect & willin product
of society's Xperimentation in dehumanization.

ya'see/ya'see

. . . message for religious brothers that are hung up . . .
. . . on so called good english . . .

>ya'see/ya'see
>crawlin
>walkin
>skippin
>runnin

however i go/whenever i go/wherever i go
somebody's always pitchin & bitchin
bout what's right & what's wrong
& at one time or another
i'm hip dat ev'rybody sing dat song
>but ya'see/ya'see
would somebody politely Xplain/to O ig'rant me
>ahhh/wellll
how somebody can be pickin & choosin/rights & wrongs for
me
>now ya'see/ya'see
a dear old brother of mine (at least i'd consider as such)
say dat when i compose poetry/dat i shouldn't use profanity
so much
>but ya'see/ya'see
i always sorta figured/dat one should style his poertry as he
pleases
it's left up to him to rap about piles of shit
or dancin leaves waltzin on gentle breezes
>& ya'see/ya'see

151

frankly i disagree/with what my brother has de nerve to
  call profanity
                    ahhhh/him bein black
                  & ahhhh/me bein black
should sorta add up to a soulful fact/dat is—
we oughtta be sidesteppin whitey's rules
instead of rightin & wrongin & amendin when dat chump
gives de clues
                    ya'see/ya'see
                        starvin
                        stealin
                        schemin
                        swindlin
i came up/was brought up/& grew up
on de black folks' side of de railroad tracks
& we were usin dat so-called profanity from times way back
                    & ya'see/ya'see
if somebody thinks my language is so fuckin bad
it's because somebody thinks me bein black is somethin bad
                  so ya'see/ya'see
don't talk whitey's yardsticks & measure my rappin down
just cause i get tired of talkin like a white-collar clown
                    cause ya'see/ya'see
                        profanity is
                        a very black
                        & rebellious
                        part of me

daydreamin

. . .for aretha . . .

sittin behind
a prison fence
thinkin bout things
dat make
no kinda sense

saw an ebony ship
(full of black freedom)
come sailin in

saw oral roberts
and billy graham
gettin de holy-white-spirit
from a bottle of seagram's gin

saw de white house
bein painted black
& green & red

saw de rockefellows
& de nixons
scrubbin my floors
& makin my bed

saw tarzan
& jungle jim

& sheena
(slut of de jungle)
gettin black feet
stomped in their faces
when they came
swingin in
on de hollywood vine

saw white judges
and de fbi
& some more honky pigs
gettin wasted
(by de black seekers
of liberation)
for oppression of
some black friends of mine

sittin behind
a prison fence
servin time
& daydreamin bout things
dat make
no kinda sense
(dat
    is
        to
            white
                niggers
                    &
                        white
                            folks)

de trip

. . . in reminiscence of a natural high i once got . . .

i lay/imprisoned in this gloomy cage
sensin ah miasma of sorrow hoverin over me
threatenin to descend upon me
& smother in de agony of self-pity
my entire bein fiercely wars against it
with ah passionate shield of black rage
while my thoughts drift above & away
from this jungle called prison
soarin on an endless trip
toward dat perfection known as eternity

questions/incessantly flashin/thru my black awareness
ticktocktickin questions/dat threaten to Xplode my con-
    sciousness
because i cannot reason ah universal answer for them
searchin my wearied mind for de dawn of life
desperately reachin out to grasp who am i
theories/debatable beliefs Xist/about de origin of life
but i find no solace in any of them

uncertainly i try to rise to my feet
but i feel de monstrous white hands
of white injustice/of white hate/of white lies
cruelly pressin against my dark body
bigotedly pinnin me to ah bed of oppression

but my consciousness has ascended beyond de horrible
    white hands
& my black awarness disgustingly looks down
at de sickly pale hands
dat continue to incarnate my dark body in white confusion

& my consciousness climbs higher- higHER-HIGHER
trippin toward de beginnin/de wisdom of life
light/spectrums of lights/bathe my black awareness
in knowledge/love/wisdom/understandin
precious gems of life dat i have sought for O/so longggg
music/divine music/dat forever harmonizes
in ah sublime symphony called life
baptizes de i which has detached itself from myself
to travel de sacred trip above
ah choir of trees/ah chorus of winds
blendin together in perfect song
colorful flowers/chirpin birds/joyful humans
ah livin orchestra fillin de universe with creations of love

my consciousness O/my freed consciousness
i feel it descendin once more
fallin back into my enslaved black flesh
snatched out of de rejuvenatin abyss of peace
by de fouled hands of white madness
back to de gloomy cage
imprisoned in whitey's putrid jungle
once more i am drownin in ah flood of white racism
ah ghostly ugliness dat seems to continuously increase
O/how i resist so my liberated consciousness
can remain on de trip
O/how i resist/like hell i resist/like hell i shall resist
until dat day comes dat i can timelessly trip
from this cage of white sadness

Othello Noel

when i round

. . . a glimpse of nelson e. mcgriff . . .
   . . . who ameriku can never rehabilitate . . .
    . . . but african people must love . . .
     . . . and show new directions. . . .

when i round/i sho-Nuff gonna get down
i gonna do-it & i gonna do-it up right
ev'ryday's gonna be ah holiday
& ev'rynight's gonna be ah party night
i gonna be firin-up much drugs
& drinkin plen-TEE wine
i gonna get high as i wanna get
& makeup for somma dat lost time   (yeah)

yeah brother/jack/jim/my main man
when i round/i sho-Nuff gonna get down
i gonna get me some real fancy rags
& some Xpensive right-on shoes
yeah jack/i gonna be de cleanest thing on de set
i gonna be stylin worse than ah broke-dick mosquito with
   de blues
my fingers gonna be ornamented with costly rings
& jim/i sho-Nuff gonna sport me some mean vines
i gonna be so Xtra super fly/so Xtra goddamn sporty
(understandddd)/i gonna blow them footdraggin NIG-
GERS' minds   (yeah)

when i round/i sho-Nuff gonna get down
i gonna get me ah showcase/custommade ride
(ah marks? ah rolls royce? or ah cadillac?)
it gonna be car-pe-ted/equipped with ah bar/bed/phone
& ah stereophonic sound center/hooked-up
across de window in de back
yeah jack/my ride is sho-Nuff gonna be somethin else to
    see
it gonna be coated in 24-karat gold
trimmed in silver/with windows carved from ruby   (yeah)

when i round/i sho-Nuff gonna get down
i gonna have me a pad dat'll be de rap of soul town
it gonna have soft/plush/ankle deep/wall-to-wall carpets
& de walls gonna be painted with bright colors
colors dat are pretty/sparklin & mellow
i ain't gonna have no colors in it dat remind me
of this cold/lifeless prison
dat been splashed with coffin green & graveyard yellow
i gonna have ah stereophonic/panasonic sound center
rigged up to flow smoothly & evenly from de walls
i gonna have color tv's/sound boxes & phones in all de
    rooms
& diamond-sprinkled curtains will add splendor to de halls
i gonna have some rare/handmade furniture
artistically carved by de finest artisan in africa
to regally grace my super Xotic den
i gonna have ev'rything in my outasight pad
dat i've been denied de fuckin right to have
in this jive/square-assed pen   (yeah)

now you my ace/my tight/my partner
& you de best friend dat i ever had
so you know i ain't lyin to ya brother
when i say dat i gonna be super bad
cause i de man with de foolproof plan
i schemed & dreamed on how to be fast
so i can do-it to whitey's ass

i know how to make ah beat
& play pass de heat
turn me loose & let me holler
cause this nigger knows how to make ah dollar
& i done got/plenTEE fat stacked under my hat (yeah)

but brother/i have to admit ah plain-O natural fact
if de pigs don't waste me/i comin back
cause ya see jack/i ain't changed one bit
i faked my way thru dat rehabilitation shit
(dig-it)/no amount of fancy white rap can justify
de why of me bein ah capitalistic slave
i want ah piece of de rock/NOW . . . BEFORE . . .
not after i in ah fuckin grave
hard work alone/never made nobody rich
& never made nobody free
whitey beennnn hip to de shit
dat why he been lyin/stealin & killin thru-out history (yeah)

yeah brother/my main man/my tight
when i round/when i round
ahhhh yeahhhh/i sho-Nuff gonna get down
i gonna use these black hands to take ah piece of dat white
    rock
when i round/when i-yeahhhh/when i round
i sho-Nuff gonna get/gonna get
i gonna get down/down/down
sho-Nuff
    gonna get
        downnnn
            WHEN I ROUND

bop mister richard

. . . with warmth for richard l. worthon . . .

aw shucks man/you so *badddd*
look at you/boppin so mean thru whitey's jungle
ya left hand broke/down by ya side
ya right hand cooly swingin in backka you
left hand meanly stylin/you gotta rhythm of ya own
right hand movin up/down/you gotta rhythm of ya own
sporty soul man/you gotta rhythm of ya own
aw shucks man/you got so much rhythm
you ah whole universe filled with rhythm/de funky rhythm
    of
survival O/bop mister richard
bop bop O/bop-bop-bop/bop bop
bop mister richard

aw shucks you so grand/brotherman
got ya handsome head cocked to ya left side
ah comely/african head/ovate & divinely sculptured
ah perfect head dat bespeaks de splendor of african people
dat's right/cock it elegantly baby/cause you badddd
lean it with style baby/cause you proudddd
you bein so poor/is so proudddd
you proud cause you ah african people
& you lordly baby/you ah black King/gottamakeitness is ya
    Kingdom

you tuff/you ruff/you ah black man screamin for survival
in ameriku
O bop mister richard
bop bop O/bop-bop-bop/bop bop
bop mister richard

aw shucks man/you so together
no need for you to do any fancy revolutionary rappin
cause black people can plainly see where you comin from
they can dig by de bold rhythm of ya bop/dat you love ya
    people
no helluva rappin for you baby/cause ya blackness is ah
    fire
an invincible fire blazin with love & pride for ya african
    heritage
you got soul dat radiates from de innermost part of ya
    bones
cause ya quietly movin in ah black direction to liberate
all african people
O bop mister richard
bop bop O/bop-bop-bop/bop bop
bop mister richard

aw shucks you so evil/brotherman
you evil cause bein evil means
dat you love ev'ry precious ounce of ya africanness
you evil cause you tiredda
ah mountain of honkey oppression blockin black progres-
    sion
you evil cause black people gotta be evil in honkey ameriku
to survive
you evil cause you tiredda
bullshittin/nochangesmade/rap sessions
you evil cause you black
& black people ev'rywhere are evil with de great white lie
O/bop with ya evil self/mister richard
bop in black dignity/mister richard
bop in love for african people/mister richard
bop in de glory of africanness/mister richard

bop in de funky rhythm of livin black body art/mister richard

bop bad & mean & bold thru whitey's jungle/mister richard

bop cause you poetry/african poetry in motion/mister richard

O/bop mister richard

bop bop O/bop-bop-bop/bop bop

bop mister richard

FRANK EARL ANDREWS—

Rahway State Prison, New Jersey

Frank Earl Andrews is on the 13th year of a 55-67 year term. During the first half of those 13 years, he walked around like a half dead man, fighting, whining and raising all kinds of hell. One day he read a novel and upon completion told himself, "shit, I can do better than that!" He immediately set out to prove it, and five years later successfully edited, published and promoted a collection of prison writings from behind the walls.

GROWING UP

I guess the only way to tell a story, any story, is to start at the beginning. That would be October 31, 1937, Halloween. Somebody once said that I was born in a taxi en route to the hospital. Perhaps that explains it all.

My mother, Esther, died when I was two years old, so I never got a chance to know her. To this day I have it embedded in my mind that she ran out on me, death being no excuse. Anyway, myself and an older brother, Harold Junior, were taken to my mother's mother to live, while the old man went out in pursuit of a new lady love. I was two weeks into kindergarden when he found her. I cried when they came for us. So did my grandmother.

The new light in my father's life was monickered, Florence Cossaboon, and the name alone gives a good indication of the type of shrew she was. She was built like Burl Ives and probably would have lost to him in a beauty contest, and I knew from jump street we weren't going to hit it off too well, especially after she smothered me all up in her broad bosom, covering half of my face with her fat lips.

We moved into 711 North Third Street, with Flossie's old lady. My brother and I found ourselves lodged in an attic, along with a bunch of old trunks, an army cot and a whole lot of pigeon shit. My third day there developed into a good sample of the turn my life had taken. It came in the form of a frame-up and a kangeroo court.

I arrived home from school that day, much more intelligent from coloring blocks for six hours, and found my fam-

ily assembled in the living room; my dad, Flossie, Harold
Junior and Grandma Gums. I didn't need a Richter Scale
to know that something was getting ready to shake. Papa-
san was supposed to be at work and the fact that he wasn't
out winning the bread boded bad for somebody. He held up
a dingy looking ring.

"Why?" He said only the one word.

"Why what?" I said only the two words.

"Why did you steal your mother's ring?" the old man
asked, matter of factly.

"I didn't steal anything!" I protested, innocent like a
motherfucker. I looked at my substitute mother, whose
disbelief was apparent.

By nature I was a crying little guy, since turning into a
miniature Niagra Falls usually got me anything I wanted
from my real grandmother, so in my confusion I decided to
turn on the tears, hoping that the threat of another great
flood would make them see that an injustice was being
done. The old man did hesitate for an instant, but at that
point in time my pseudo-grandmother opened her jibs.

"It was found in his room, and it certainly didn't walk
there by itself!" She shifted her wrinkled butt around in her
chair and stared indignantly out a window, gums working
like a cud chewing cow. "I don't know what they let him
get away with over there," she sighed, meaning my real
grandmother, "but it is obvious they did a poor job of raising him this far."

If there was ever a person in my life that cared about
me, it was my real grandmom, and even at that stage of
my life I wasn't about to let no shrunk-up hag talk about
her. For a second or two I contemplated between running
out of the house to my grandmom's or handling it on the
spot myself. I opted for the latter, which proved to be my
downfall.

"Don't you talk about her!"

The old man's hesitation was over. He sprang out of his
chair and backhanded me in the mouth. After I slid across
the wooden floor on my little fundament, I thought about
telling him that two people lived in that damned attic, but

before I could shake the first batch of sparks from my head, my dad was on me again. I only had time to cover up.

Most of his shots landed on my arms and legs, but one time I peeked out of my little ball and got grunched square in the mouth. I was then dragged to my feet and catapulted up the stairs by a big knee in my ass.

Junior showed up after dark with a stolen peanut butter sandwich. I figured he was experiencing guilt pangs, since he was the only other soul living in the attic. I couldn't eat the sandwich anyway, as earlier I had picked a tooth from my lower lip and it was sore as hell. Even then it wasn't my nature to tell on anyone, though innumerable times I had to fight down an urge to knock Junior's eyeball loose while he slept. Yet, he was much bigger than me and on prior occasions and run-ins, I had eventually to run for my life. However, an opportunity for vengeance (in another manner) presented itself a few days later.

Twice a week, Junior and myself took our baths in the same tub at the same time. Usually, I ended up squeezed at one end, while he spread out and did a "Willie the Whale" act; ducking under and coming up spitting out a geyser of bath water. On this particular occasion, I watched him go into his aqua-bag, delighted to no end each time he came up spouting. Only I knew that an unusually long stream of piss had been unleashed into his private ocean.

Neither Flossie nor my dad wanted to run the risk of explaining my banged-up face, so they kept me out of school for a couple of weeks. By the time I once again picked up on my education, I had a completely new outlook on life and a lot of things bugged me, such as wearing punky knickers while all the other little guys wore long pants; going to bed before dark and missing all the good stories on the radio. The main thing that got my hackles up was not being allowed to go to the movies on Saturdays, unless Junior came along as chaperone. Even then I couldn't go until I had cleaned a cellar the size of Convention hall. Furthermore, I despised the constant diet of cabbage and spinach because if I wanted an eyedropper of pudding or a minis-

cule piece of cake, I had to choke down mountains of the
gook. Another grievance dealt with pesos and I didn't feel
that a fair share of nickels and dimes came my way. Finally, since I had been labeled a duck, I decided to start
quacking.

The first thing I did was devise a method of getting
around the yukky edibles. When no one was paying me any
mind, I simply grabbed a gob of whatever proteinous shrub
happened to be on my plate, squeezed the juice out of it
and put it in my pocket. This worked out pretty cool because I was still in that age of adolescence where peed
pants wasn't an outrage. Thus, I had an ideal cover-up
for the wet spots that constantly showed up. A change of
day to day apparel was my second priority. For that I
would need some financial assistance, and my idea where
and how to get it concurred with what they thought of me
around that house.

Guiffra's was a small confectionary, in the heart of Millville's business district, which wasn't saying too much because the main drag was only six blocks long. I passed the
rear of the store every day on my way to and from Censor
School, and I couldn't help noticing a piece of cardboard
where the glass window should have been. Even had I not
been an oppressed little kid—the guy was asking for it.

Naturally, I couldn't strike during the daylight hours, so
that meant waiting till after dark, which also meant I would
have to launch off from the attic, as I was sent there the
minute the sun faded in the west. I waited until I thought
everyone was sacked out, including Big Bro, then climbed
through the window onto the porch roof. It was an easy
slide down the drainpipe to the ground.

Getting into Guiffra's was the easiest part of the operation and I accomplished this by pushing in the cardboard. It
took me some time to locate the cash register in the dark,
and longer to figure which key opened the mother. I damn
near pooped myself when the register drawer finally did
jangle open. Eventually I recovered my wits, took off one
of my socks and filled it with moola, mostly small change. I
then ate an assortment of sweets until my tummy bulged,

jammed the sock in my back pocket, climbed out and waddled back to the Cossaboon Spread. Five minutes later I was up the drainpipe and on the porch roof. As I pulled my back leg over the window sill, the lights flashed on.

There they were! The grand jury, sitting around the room in silence, jaws tight, facial muscles working, paragons of law and order. The only one who didn't look like he wanted to piss in my face was my brother, and his earlier exploits explained why he wasn't hostile.

"Where the hell you been?" The old man sat on a dusty trunk.

"Outside playing . . ." Even at that age, I knew my response sounded like bullshit.

Flossie reclined regally on a straight-backed chair, where both cheeks of her wide ass hung over the sides of the seat. She gave a little caustic laugh. "At two o'clock in the morning, you were outside playing?"

My old man ran a worried hand through his hair. He shook his head from side to side. "I don't know what I'm going to do with you, Frank."

Granny Cossaboon had some ideas. She stopped chewing her cud long enough to voice one. "I know what you *should* do!"

A butt beating appeared imminent and the hoplessness of the situation brought the tears. I didn't really believe that bawling would get me a reprieve, but what else was there to do? Perhaps it was the tears, perhaps my dad felt an asswhupping wouldn't serve any purpose, perhaps he realized that I was *his* son and that it was between us and not the whole damn world. Whatever, I felt pretty good when he ran the old lady, her old lady and Junior, downstairs. When we were alone, he looked at me sort of sad-like and rose from the trunk.

"Go to bed, Frank. Junior'll sleep on the couch."

I don't remember, before or after, ever feeling closer to my father. I cried harder, fighting down the urge to come clean. . . . I was torn with indecision as he came over and put his thick arms around me, hugging me real close. At this juncture, my knickers failed, slid down my butt and hit the floor with a thonk. Silver and copper jumped out of the sock and scattered all over the floor. In the instant before confusion cleared, I almost managed to squirm from my fathers embrace, but the knickers twisted around my legs dumped me down. Great googamooga! The ensuing ass-whipping defies description.

Things settled down a bit after that. My booty was confiscated and I never heard any more about Guiffra's. Flossie blew up fatter than a Brahma bull and in no time I had a half-sister named Jean-Marie. My father got a new job at Dupont's in Deepwater, New Jersey, and we left Grandma Gums and her gang for a new home. Golf Manor sprawled a few miles from Deepwater, with the main focus of the housing development being a huge 18-hole golf course. We lived at 52 Manor Avenue in a pretty blue and white brick house, with plenty of front lawn and a huge back yard. It was twice as nice as the rat hole in Millville and I especially liked the idea of Junior and me actually having our own bedroom. Yeah, things were copesetic, and it even looked like Flossie was beginning to like me a little. It didn't take long for the novelty of the baby and the new house to wear off though, and pretty soon we were back to normal: If I wanted to go to the movies on Saturday, I had to clean a cellar the size of Madison Square Garden, mow a lawn bigger than Central Park and tidy up a back yard the size of the Orange Bowl. I received a quarter as reimbursement for my labor, but felt grossly underpaid as it cost fourteen cents for the movie, five cents for the bus to Pennsgrove where the theater was and five cents back, leaving me a measly penny for refreshments. Adding insult to injury was my Big Bro. He didn't do a damn thing, yet I couldn't go to the movies unless he took me.

Since there was only one living being around that I could whup, I transferred my rage to him. His name was Blackie and he was a cat. It wasn't all unjustified, those drum-ups I meted out, because that scrawny, feline freak, with a white stripe running down the middle of his face, didn't do nothing but strut around all day, drink milk and shit in the cellar I had to clean. One Saturday in particular, I decided to show him that it would be a risky proposition for him to continue using the cellar for an outhouse. It was easy to catch him, as he was a greedy little prick, and the minute I held out a piece of left-over lunch meat he ran up and practically clawed my fingers off getting to it. I let him savor his prize a bit, rubbing his back, until I had him purring like a super-charged diesel. It was all over for him as I snatched his scruffy neck and jammed him into a burlap bag. I secured the top and tied the sack to a water pipe, then went into a Sugar Ray Robinson crouch and started firing left hooks and right hands. For a long time after that, there was one son-of-a-bitch in that house that respected Frank Earl Andrews. Everytime Blackie saw me coming, he cut out the other way, *muy pronto!*

My first real run-in with the courts came a few months later. It was more of an impulsive action than anything else. On one side of our house was a patch of waist-high grass. This was my main hang-out, with a home-made rifle, sniping everything that came into range. I was scoping in on the milkman's brisket, but held up on my trigger finger when he deposited a huge leather bag on the dashboard of his truck. He climbed out, not even bothering to slide the door closed, and headed for my house. I let him get inside, took a quick survey, then sped for the truck. In one quick swoop I snatched up the bag and sprinted back to the safety of my jungle. I laid on my stomach, breathless, until I heard the truck pull away. For a long time after that I just stared at the bulging bag. I was rich! The bag was loaded!

Crime does have some drawbacks, and this particular caper wasn't any exception. Her name was Betsy Boyd. When she evidenced herself, I was on the way to my cellar door, holding the bag low on my side.

"What's in the bag?"

Betsy was the offspring of Ed and Margaret Boyd, a couple who lived next door. Up to that point me and the little blonde had been pretty cool. She was two years older than me, and the *only* fluff permitted in my secret jungle. She was okay for a girl, I thought. At the moment though, I was scared and in one helluva hurry.

"None of your damn business!"

I made as if to go past her, but she grabbed my arm. She must have felt pretty sure of herself because we had long ago settled who was the toughest. "I saw you steal that bag from the milk truck."

I was on the verge of smacking the shit out of her, but she stopped me cold. Scared damn near to death, I made a complete about face.

"Okay! I'll give you half."

She still hesitated and for a few seconds it looked like her only objective was to rat on me. Presently she grabbed my hand and led me back to the side of the house. Wasn't nothing but a party after that. We dumped the loot out, a billion dollar mountain of nickels, dimes, quarters and half dollars. We ran our hands through it, poured it on each other, giggled, laughed, bubbled. Later, we divided up the money. The next day the roof fell in on "The Great Milk Truck Robbery".

One of my favorite haunts was a pond near the golf course, where I caught miniature turtles for sale to the five and dime in Pennsgrove, and stray golf balls which I cleaned off and sold for fifty cents each. I was knee deep in muddy water when Ed Boyd stopped his car on the road nearby. He called me to the car and told me my father wanted me at home. As we rode, I sort of knew what was up. Ed didn't say anything, but he didn't have to. The minute I stepped into the living room I knew for certain the jig was up. Betsy sat on the sofa next to her mother, Margaret, who was damn near a double to Flossie; fat and bloppy. Betsy was crying uncontrollably, but rather than feeling any compassion for her, I felt hate and anger. If she would have minded her own damn business, neither one of us would have been in any trouble. Her sniveling affected me in another way though, and I made up my mind then and there not to cry like that. No one was going to make me. Ed closed the door and nudged me to the center of the room.

"Here he is, Had." Ed sounded like he'd just rounded up Jesse James.

My dad and Flossie sat in occasional chairs at opposite ends of the sofa. On a coffee table in front of the sofa was the leather bag and a variety of toys. That stupid-assed Betsy! She didn't even have enough sense to hide the stuff she bought.

"Where'd that come from?" My dad motioned to the coffee table.

I shrugged.

"Goddammit!" he shouted, half coming out of his chair. "When I ask you a question, I want a damn answer! Where did you get that bag of money?"

It was evident that my old man was fighting his temper. The only thing that probably restrained him was the presence of the Boyd's. I looked at Betsy again. Her haggard appearance only strengthened my resolve not to let them make me like that.

"I never saw it before."

Everyone in the room knew I was lying. Flossie couldn't keep her mouth shut, but I hadn't really expected her to.

"How did that bag of money get in your dresser?"

I shrugged, and the old man blew his cool entirely. "You little piece of shit!" He jumped up and grabbed a handful of my shirt, like a muscle-man for the syndicate. "I've had enough of you, bub! Now, tell me who you stole that money from, or I'm going to beat your head down through your asshole!"

I was scared, so much so that a stream of warm piss started trailing down my leg. Another glance at Betsy reinforced my earlier vow. I shook my head, and that got me a smack in the chops. My dad turned to Betsy.

"Where'd he steal the money from?"

Betsy just looked at him, and I could swear I detected the hint of a smile on her pretty little face.

"Had asked you a question!" Margaret hissed through her teeth.

"I don't know," Betsy mumbled.

That got her a slap in the jibs, but she just sniffled and continued to look at me.

Ed leaned against the wall, near the door. "She told us earlier that he stole it from the milk truck."

"Is that the truth?" my dad asked me, still clutching my shirt with his big hand.

I didn't even answer the motherfucker, and I think the look of pure hate on my face caused him to throw me bodily across the room. He picked up the telephone and called the police.

Judge Rustling S. Leap had a gentle look about him. He wore a full head of white hair and spoke in a soft voice. I wasn't afraid of him because he seemed to be genuinely interested in me. I stood in front of his desk, flanked on both sides of my parents.

"What do you think we should do?" Judge Leap asked my father.

"We can't do anything with him, your honor," Flossie volunteered.

I looked up at my dad. He looked away.

"Do you think a few months away might help?" This was directed at my father also.

"Something has to be done!" Flossie put in, once again taking the initiative. "We've tried everything!"

I didn't pay much attention to the rest of it. I really didn't give a good fuck. Maybe a change *would* do me good.

"That State Home for Boys is a nice place, Frank. You'll have a lot of boys your own age to play with, and they have movies, a swimming pool, even a boy scout camp. You keep your nose clean and I promise to have you home before school starts."

I didn't cry then, though I wanted to, but not because I was going away. I knew from the moment I met her that Florence Cossaboon wasn't my mother and never would be. What made me want to cry was the fact that I didn't have a father either. That made me want to cry, but I didn't, never again in my life!

GROWN UP

or

WHATEVER HAPPENED TO FRANK ANDREWS?

(see over!)

HIDDEN-GUN
BANDIT
SHOOTS COP
—KIDNAPS 2

By JOE O'DOWD

A holdup man, who concealed a gun from police during 40 hours of custody, shot an undersheriff in South Jersey last night, kidnapped two other men and forced them to take him to midcity Philadelphia, where he disappeared.

The fugitive, who told his hostages that "nobody is going to put me in jail for 20 years," is Frank E. Andrews, 24, of Chestnut St., Millville, N.J. He's armed with a .22 caliber pistol.

*Philadelphia Daily News—July 22, 1962

MILLVILLE ESCAPEE'S BRAGGING OVER

Cops Nab Man In Phila.,

Get His Gun This Time

PHILADELPHIA (AP) — Police arrested a gun-toting escaped prisoner Saturday as he made a telephone call in a center city bus terminal while over 100 persons waited to go to the seashore.

Frank Andrews, 24, Millville, one bullet still in his pistol — he had emptied four others into a New Jersey constable Friday night in making his escape—was seized during a struggle with five officers.

Bandit on Outs

With Girl Aide

Andrews' 'Moll' Found

Two Sides To Frank

By JIM NEVILLE

Love, love and the world well lost . . .
Who wrote that?
Well, it doesn't matter, but it aptly fits the case of a 23-year old mother who left her three children and went off with a hardened criminal.

*AP—July 22, 1962
*Pennsville Record—July 24, 1962

Pleads Guilty to Eight Charges

Andrews Sentencing

Tomorrow Faces Life

By "Dusty" Rhodes

Pennsville — If anyone ever broke the laws of God and man it was Frank Andrews, 24, of Millville. If anyone was ever given every consideration of his legal rights and day in court it was this same man. This convict, robbed, kidnapped, assaulted and escaped. He defied those in authority, yet when his chance came in two courts with in two days, he smilingly pleaded guilty to eight charges.

Failed, Now Jailed

Andrews, Held On 8 Counts;

GOP Charges 'Bungling' in Andrews Case

*Pennsville Progress—August 3, 1962

Andrews Draws 41-47 Years In
State Prison

No Emotion Shown
At Long Sentence

Salem — Showing the same stoic manner, Frank Earl Andrews, 24, kidnapper, gunman, thief accepted the sentence of 41-47 years handed down by Judge Alvin R. Featherer in Salem County Court last week, with no emotion. His only request was to "get out of this place soon as I can". The judge promised he would be moved as "expeditiously as possible", and he was; within one hour the criminal was on his way to New Jersey State Prison.

*Camden Courier—August 4, 1962

God Might Be A Midget

God might be a midget
   in more respects than one.
Else why isn't the world a Camelot
   where gloom never covers the sun?

Why Waterloo? Why World War Two?
   Why places like Wounded Knee?
Why are some wrong? Why are some strong?
   Why isn't freedom free?

Why so much hate? Why Watergate?
   Why Attica? Why My Lai?
Why disease and poverty?
   Why do babies die?

Why enemies and vendettas?
   Why guns? Why prey? Why hunted?
Why if "he" built this place called earth,
   Why isn't it like "he" wanted?

It just might be possible
   that perhaps "he's" not so small!
Could be with all these goings-on
   "he" might not be at all!

COUNTRY CLUBS

ON VARIOUS OCCASIONS
   I HAVE HEARD THE DECLARATION
   THAT PRISONS ARE BEING TURNED
   INTO COUNTRY CLUBS

YET I WOULD DONATE
   THE NEXT CREATURE
   I TRAP IN MY OATMEAL
   TO THE SMITHSONIAN INSTITUTE
   JUST TO SEE
   ONE OF THE DECRIERS
HAVING TO EAT SPAGHETTI
   WITH A SPOON
TRYING TO WATCH TELEVISION
   IN A ROOM WITH FIFTY OTHER GUYS
BEING FORCED TO LIVE
   ONE FOOT AWAY FROM A MOTHERFUCKER
   SO FILTHY
   THAT HIS FALSE TEETH
   HAVE CAVITIES!

AN ODE TO THAT GOOD STUFF

Ain't had none in ages
Needin' some real bad
Wish I could just touch it
Before I go mad

Hope I ain't forgot how to do it
Wouldn't that be a shame
Finally gettin' to it
Comin' up lame

Right now I'll settle for a guarantee
So I'll know definitely
That some will be waitin'
If they ever set me free

I pray it's still somethin' special
'Cause at just any ole thang I will scoff
But if nobody won't give me none
I'm gonna saw mine off

THE BUNTLINE SPECIAL

I have never been hurt like this before. It is a fire, a hellish inferno, that consumes and blots out all else. I never understood why I was selected for such an agony, to experience such terror. Perhaps in the last few minutes of my life I can recount it to you. But I must hurry . . .

The day began sunny and a soft breeze blew in from the south. I was walking, just strolling along and enjoying the fact that I was alive and free, and able to bask in the glory of such a fine day. Several times I stopped, but merely to window shop, as in my haste to get away from the antiseptic-smelling hospital I had left my wallet behind.

I came upon a little sports shop. It was a small place, dingy, gray, ugly, situated between one of those new high-rise department stores and an elegant nightclub. The building itself reminded me of a weed, about to be smothered by two giant roses. I never noticed the shop before, though I must have passed it many times while escorting my wife to work. She was employed as a secretary for a law firm down the street.

I stopped at the sports shop, casually admiring the assortment of outdoor gear, and my gaze fell on a revolver near the rear of the display window. There was nothing unusual about this particular weapon, other than an extraordinarily long barrel. I found myself staring at it, fascinated by the blue, almost black, merchant of death. Without realizing it, I was going into the shop.

A tiny bell tinkled my arrival, and an ancient individual

hobbled around a glass counter to greet me. His smile was a dark hole surrounded by purple gums; his hair was nearly gone, with only a few strands left behind gnarled and wrinkled ears. I ventured a guess at his age, but gave up quickly —he could've been anywhere from fifty to a hundred or more years old.

"Affanoon," he said in a drawl. His voice sounded like air hissing from a punctured tire.

"Afternoon."

"Sump'n I kin do fer ya?"

"That revolver in the . . ."

"The one in the winder." It was a statement, not a question.

I nodded, wondering what the hell I was doing. I had no intention of buying any damn gun!

"Not fer sale," the old man drawled. "Don't know why I don't sell 'er, no pertickler reason I kin think of." His mouth worked, like a fish sucking for air. "Wanna see 'er up close?"

Before I had a chance to say yes or no the old man was by the display window, lifting the gun out. When he returned, he carried the aged revolver in his wrinkled hands, holding it in front of him almost reverently.

"Just an ole Buntline Special. Wanna load 'er up, see how she's balanced?"

I didn't want to load the friggin thing! And once I had the feel of the icy steel in my hands, I wanted to drop it and flee into the street. But I stood there, watching as the old man reached under the counter for a box of .44 cartridges.

I had never used a pistol before, but I found myself handling the Buntline Special like an expert. The old man had a smile plastered on his antique face as I loaded the cylinder. The smile began to fade after I snapped the cylinder shut and pointed the gun at his chest. The smile was still there when a .44 slug slammed into his frail frame and drove him halfway over the counter.

With a taste of horror in my throat and stomach, I gaped at the rumpled heap. I tried to open my hand, so the gun

Othello Noel

could fall, but my fingers no longer seemed to be a part of me and I could not release the accursed revolver.

I rushed outside. A woman passing by gave me a startled look, then began to run. The Buntline Special roared, and her running days were over. A blue-shirted policeman, gun drawn, raced toward me in a crouch. At thirty feet a bullet ripped through his shirt pocket, retiring him from the force.

A crowd of people formed, milled about, across the street. The Buntline tugged me toward them at a run, made me laugh hysterically as the frightened figures scurried away like a swarm of scared sewer rats.

Unaware of how I arrived there, I found myself in front of the office building where my wife worked. If I could get to her, she would help me get free from the fiendish Buntline Special.

I took the stairs two at a time. When I swung open the office door, her mouth fell open in surprise and fear. I tried to speak, to tell her of the horrible trip the Buntline Special was taking me on, the things it was making me do, but no words came out. Instead, the revolting revolver exploded in my hand and she flew backwards, flopping limply into a corner. Tears flowed and through them I spat a million curses at the evil weapon, wondering when the ugly lump of steel would be done with me. But not yet! The incredible pistol forced my hand inward, twisting my wrist, until the long barrel was jammed into my mid-section. I pleaded, I cried, begging the demon who devised such a nightmare to release me. My supplications were to no avail because my finger began to tighten on the trigger. I braced myself, but how can one brace himself for death?

The bullet tore through my insides, scorching, lancing, aching. After that, the damnable Buntline Special clung only for an instant more, then fell away to the floor.

Through a rapidly descending veil of obscurity, I am looking at it now, wondering what it was that so overpowered me. At this moment it is simply a blob of metal, a relic from a dead age.

Perhaps this is only a nightmare, and the distant wail of police sirens is a part of it. Perhaps I am mad, and that is what you are probably thinking. Well, madness is the price of immortality and greatness. Name another whose armies swept across Europe with such fury! Name another who rose from a manure heap to a kingship! Name a name that equals that of Napoleon Bonaparte!

My God! I am dying! What a way for an emperor to go! It hurts to even think about it anymore, so I am going to change and be something much simpler, like a giant 175-pound walnut. That way I can just sit and laugh, while the squirrels try to figure out how to drag me up into one of their tree holes . . .

Othello Noel

STRAIGHT AHEAD

Him who always looks downward
  Might get banged from the top
    Of a low-slung doorway
While the man who stares at the skies
  Will probably stumble
    Over the dung-heap of life.
Eyes straight ahead is the wisest course
  And that way
    You only have to worry about the sides.

THE GREAT DISCOVERY

I once thought I was a genius
another Einstein
waiting to discover
the theory of relativity
   or Newton's law of gravitation
   or Torricelli's barometer
   or Franklin's bifocals.
Yet
   no amazing revelation
   did I ever
   contribute to mankind.
However
   after thirty-six years
   I have stumbled upon
   a monumental discovery:
If my brains could be transferred
to a bluebird
he would immediately do
a one-and-a-half somersault
loop up his own butt
and break his goddamn neck!

DISNEYLAND

THERE AREN'T MANY
  WHO CONSIDERED
  WALT DISNEY
  TO BE IN THE GENRE
OF
  REMBRANDT
  PICASSO
OR
  VAN GOGH
BUT
  HE WAS AN ARTIST
  AND USING OL' AMERICA
  AS A SUBJECT
  HE GAVE US
    DIS
      NEY
        L
          A
            N
              D!

LESLIE VAN HOUTEN—

California Institution for Women

In accord with saving the best for last, we have followed suit here, and think you will find the writings of this sensitive little thoroughbred worthy of many raves. She too lived in the shadow of the gas chamber, but with a surprising resiliency she refused to let it numb her and set about turning the dreariness of life in prison to her advantage. Leslie is in tune with the planet, smelling extra deep of the fragrance in a rose or dreaming dreams of the desert and the sea, or even finding flavor in the dryness of a cardboard-tasting institutional dinner. She never wrote a word for publication in her life, but fortunately she did this time, so we are all rolling in good fortune because of it.

IMA FIBBON

"Come with me", a uniformed officer directed.

A steel gate rolled open, then shut behind us. My first impression was that I had entered Fort Knox, but no, it was the county jail and judging by my escorts' iceberg features, I knew I wasn't going to be treated like a gold bar. "Welp," I told myself, "better prepare for the trip of your life, goilie." With that in mind I took a deep breath and forced my chin up. What the hell! Worst could happen was I'd get it bent back down.

Being booked was frantic and confusing. "Birthday . . . Age . . . Last address . . . Name . . . sput sput sput brp brp brp . . ."

"Ima Fibbon . . . Eighty-five . . . Apollo Eleven . . ."

"Wrist!" An I.D. bracelet was clamped on my extended wrist. I was born again—439126.

A pointed finger directed me around a corner. "Strip." I removed my clothing. "Bend over and spread your legs." While my ovaries were inspected, I tried to escape the smothering reality of the situation, by thinking of myself as Citation, being prepared for the Kentucky Derby. It was impossible to drift away for long though, and the venomous sounding commands dragged me back. "Follow me".

Another room. Another officer. This woman looked like Night Train Lanes' daddy. "Get in the tub."

Conscious of my nakedness, I lowered myself into three inches of water, after banging my knee on the side of the tub. I splashed a bit, mostly going through the motions. I was much too nervous to miss my rubber ducky.

Two sets of unfeeling eyes watched as I stepped out. Night Train spun me around like a top, while Iceberg Face sprayed me all over with insecticide, from a hose attached to the wall. Making a final attempt at dignity, I tried pretending that I was a stringbean plant and that the farmers were trying to keep the insects from eating my leaves.

"Your dress." Night Train handed me a folded bundle. The dress was constructed out of faded blue denim, with a big "L" on the front. I figured it must be one of Night Trains' seconds, because it hung over me like a tent. It stuck in places, but that was probably because no one had seen fit to give me a towel and I was soaking wet.

The sweater they gave me was definitely a fugitive from a nursery school, because it ended right at the elbows and just a few inches below the bust; definitely no wash and wear! The rubber thongs that served as shoes were also miniscule, and I knew at first glance they would never be able to deal with my moon men. Hoping they would exchange them for a larger size, I inquired about the possibility. I should have checked with Jimmy the Greek first, then I'd have known the odds were a zillion to one against such a consideration.

"Wear that! We aren't running Macy's!"

Iceberg Face pointed a gnarled finger at a seat in front of a glaring light and a whole lot of photographic equipment. I sat down, grinning like a Chesire Cat. "Don't smile! This isn't for the cover of Cosmopolitan!"

No wonder all the post office mug shots looked so rough. Nobody said cheese, or even held up a little birdie.

Fingerprints followed the mug shots and by the time we were finished my nails had been beaten down to stubbles. To top it off, my cigarettes were all gone. I was near tears, because I knew that place wasn't going to be my friend.

"Birthday ... Age ... Last address ... Name ... Sput sput sput brp brp brp . . ."

"Ima Fibbon . . . Eighty-five . . . Apollo Eleven . . ."

"Follow me, Ima Fibbon!" Night Train tucked the football under her arm and headed up-field. She stopped at an elevator. There we joined a group of other "fish."

The next stop was the infirmary and a nurse with more questions than Carter had little liver pills. "Pneumonia? Parkinson's Disease? Leprosy? Peanut Butterbulocis? Birthday . . . Age . . . Last address . . . Name . . ."

"Ima Fibbon . . . Eighty-five . . . Apollo Eleven . . . Can I have an aspirin? I'm starting to feel like a hypochondriac."

"You'll feel a lot worse in the hole if you don't button your trap," said Florence Nightingale sweetly, before disappearing in a swish of white.

The next stop on the itinerary was the tank. We marched in twos and I was just getting into the ol' esprit de corps when we reached our destination. The hike was over. We wuz home at last!

The tank was made up of twelve cells, enclosed in a barred compound, sort of a dozen little cells surrounded by one big one. The front of each cell was in fact a sliding door, which was also constructed out of bars. The only outside light flowed in through a row of windows adjacent to a catwalk that ran the length of the tier. Behind the row of residences ran the electrical and sewage lines, the latter being obvious via the funky odors that filtered through a small vent in the rear of each cell. The tank officer opened the tier gate and as each fish passed through, Night Train handed her a granny sleeping gown, a sheet, and a mattress cover, all made out of muslin.

"Ima Fibbon"?

"Yes."

"Cell twelve."

Twelve was the last in line and during my brief stroll to my new adobe hacienda I sent my mind out on one of its excursions, the kind that never let me fully escape for long, but which did provide a respite now and then. This time I opted for Ali Baba, but before I could say "open Sesame", the door thundered wide. The cell could have easily passed for a cave, but I didn't see any treasure lying around. My mind came back at that point, and it dawned on me that I would be spending the night in a cage with two complete strangers.

I made a quick assessment of the cell. There were only two bunks, and since they were occupied with two beings who were occupied with the jails' most popular pastime—zzzzzing—I assumed the mat on the floor belonged to little ol' me. When I dragged the pallet out from under the bottom bunk, one of my roomies muttered something which sure didn't sound like a greeting. A few minutes later, as I spread my linen over the mattress, I found that my original thought had been correct.

"C'mon with all that goddamn noise, girl! Jesus Christ! Trying to get some fucking sleep!"

I sat down on my unmade-up mattress, but remained awake, trying to figure out some solution to the million and one questions that floated in and out of my head. They were still floating when the harshly-lit county jail greeted the dusky dawn.

I decided to announce that I had never been in the slammer before, and that I hoped my cell-mates would overlook any breeches of etiquette I might commit. I received a few grunts and sidelong glances for my efforts, making me more aware only of the fact that I was just a dumb, scared, dizzy hippy who would be better off keeping her mouth shut. I climbed off my regal sack, slid it under the bottom cot, and sat on the floor by the door, waiting for whatever came next. I didn't have long to wait, and damn near had a miscarriage when the twelve doors opened in unison, almost catching the hem of my denim tent in the process. I thought, surely *that* rumble would measure at least six points on the Richter Scale.

"One step out and halt!"

The command came from a new officer, or at least a different one from the guard who had tucked us in. She wasn't a bad looking woman, except for an exaggerated bra that made her mammaries stick out like two torpedoes, and a young face that was tight. Her words were clipped.

She waited for us to line up in front of our cells before starting her orientation. "There is to be no talking in the dining area. Anyone caught with her mouth open, except for eating, will lose her meal and end up in lock-up. Upon returning from the dining area, you will go immediately to your cells and stand facing them. Do not talk or your doors will not be opened and you will remain standing at attention, until *I* feel the inclination to let you in. Is that perfectly clear?" The last was ridiculous. How could it be otherwise?

The mode of travel going to and from the mess hall was in pairs. By now everyone knew who they would double up with, except me. Pairing was usually white on white, black on black, with an occasional sprinkling of salt and pepper. While I stood there, like a new kid on the block, the others fell into line. I was getting a bit apprehensive, when a tall woman with a short afro motioned for me to stand next to her. She was the tank trustee and I smiled my gratitude, not giving a damn that her skin was the color of deep chocolate. She smiled back and I felt a lot better.

The advantage of pairing with the trustee meant marching at the front of the line. As we started off I turned myself into a wagon-train scout. Searching from side to side, I made certain no bandits were lurking in the underbrush, crouching in ambush on our wagon-train. My vigilance got us through the pass and into the mess hall safely. Here, masses of women in blue herded masses of prisoners in and out, amid the sounds of bashing metal trays, clanking spoons and shouting guards.

"Keep that line moving! Shut your trap! Eyes to the front! Yip yip yip . . . Move along little doggie . . . Ki yi yippee yi yi . . ."

The mess hall could hold about one hundred and fifty women, but using the shuttle method with people constantly rotating in and out, a population of about six hundred female souls ate in the space of an hour. The line filed along one wall, passing first a tray rack, then a kitchen worker who handed out spoons. Across an aluminum counter, food was slapped onto the trays by a varying shade of inmate arms, belonging to blank and empty faces. Diners then moved between rows of four-set dinette tables, sat down and started scoffing mucho fasto. Eating time ranged between ten and fifteen minutes, making it apparent that *Amy Vanderbilt's Book Of Etiquette* wasn't written with prisoners in mind. If one was to be full, speed was the order of the day, perpetual motion by both spoon and lips. Otherwise a resident could find herself marching out with tears in her eyes and a protesting stomach.

I had always wondered if the James Cagney/George Raft prison movies were mostly put-ons, but I soon learned that there was much authenticity in the shifting of eyes without turning the head. To a basketball player, this is known as "lateral vision", but when mentioned in association with people behind bars it is called "sleazy-eyed." Yet, by making little slits out of my eyes, I found that I could peek around at will without being detected, thus get a glimpse of what was going on—hundreds of eyes peering like mine, hundreds of prisoners talking, but not one pair of lips moving. I especially noted the numerous affirmative nods and hand signals to my partner, and I felt good about that, more secure, sort of "in like Flynn."

"You dumb honky bitch!" a loud voice erupted suddenly. "Don't you never put your nasty white paws in my cup! How the hell do I know where your hand's been at?"

The activity turned instantly into silence. I held my breath. A riot? And they didn't even know my mama's phone number! But my fears were groundless, because without a word of admonishment, an officer brought the culprit another cup. Soon, spoons were clanking away again, as if nothing had ever happened.

Two beeps and a bop later we were on the way out of the mess hall, moving first in single file so that an officer at the door could make sure each woman turned in a spoon, then in pairs again for the march back to the tier.

Hut-two-three-four. Hut-two-three-four. Hut-two-three

four. Ain't no use in looking down. Hut-two-three-four.
Ain't no discharge on the ground. Hut-two-three-four.

The tier gate banged shut behind us, and we waited in
front of our cells. Everyone was eager for a return to the
slammers. Bullet Breast had other ideas.

"Now really, ladies," she scolded like a schoolmarm, "the
line returning from the dining area was a shambles. I
warned you earlier that if you persisted in acting like juve-
niles, then you could expect to be treated like same. Let's
see if you are mature enough to remain quiet for the next
twenty minutes."

The keys jangled away and ironically on cue the squawk
box over our heads began emitting music. After a few bars
of "just a little lovin', early in the mawnin'" frayed nerves
gave way first with a hissed, "that bitch", then a disgusted,
"what a motherfucker", finally topped off with a weary,
"shit, I'm tired."

The versatile vocabulations, all referring to B.B., were
phenomenal in that during a twenty minute period she was
called every low name in the English language without one
repetition. There was even a "puta" thrown in for good
measure. Then the ring of returning keys cut all of that off.
Like tin soldiers we tightened ranks and when Generalissi-
mo B.B. rounded the bend she beamed with satisfaction.

"All right, ladies. Maybe next time you'll do better." She
was about to swing the doors, when the third woman on my
left decided to let loose with a few things that had been
overlooked.

"Trouble with you bitch is you ain't grinning and walking bowlegged. Just because your dude's a fag don't mean
you pozed to bring your attitude in here on us."

Naturally, Penelope de Bust responded to the outburst.
"Perhaps the lady with the foul mouth will be honest
enough to repeat that to my face."

From further down the line: "Ain't no Abe Lincoln's
here, woman!"

After the titter died away, B.B. locked the control box
and delivered another slap on the wrist, probably designed

to alienate us from the girls who had done the talking.
"Stay there then, until I find out who the guilty parties are."

She jangled away and the legionnaires slumped. I was
definitely tired, but I felt good behind the fact that no one
had given up our loud-mouthed comrades, even though we
all wanted to strangle them. An hour later the doors rum-
bled open.

I waited until my roomies had tumbled back into their
sacks, then brushed the violin-sized footprints off my mattress. Before I could flop a guard appeared on the outside
catwalk.

"Ima Fibbon . . . Ollra pua . . . Ellca onea . . . Opta
unkba . . ." Good thing I understood Pig-Latin, because
that sure was the way the instructions were spewed out.
However, the news was pleasing, since three people in that
can was kinda tight, a sho 'nuf case against putting them
little ol' fishies in a can. The thought of my own bed made
me light-headed, on equal terms with a kid who just received an all-day sucker from the dentist in return for not
biting his finger. In one quick motion I swooped up my
bedding and belongings and backed out the door, which
had been deadlocked open. I felt a momentary pang of
gratitude for my roomies, since neither one of them had
stepped on my head during the night, so I hesitated long
enough to say "adios amigos."

I should have known better. "Goodbye motherfucker!"
one of them growled, as glad to be rid of me as I was glad
to be gotten rid of.

On feet with wings I floated down the freeway, tempted
to do a few pirouettes. Because of the precarious grip on
my bundle I gave the dance a second thought and instead
hummed along with the radio. "You got me going in circles
. . ." At the same time I counted down the cells under my
breath . . . seven . . . six . . . five . . . four . . ."
BLUMP!

"Watch where the fuck you're going!"

Actually, the contact was the other driver's fault, as I
was on the freeway and she had darted from the third cell,

like coming out of a side street without first checking traffic on the turnpike. Yet she was built like Sonny Liston and since I hadn't received any black belts in karate, I figured diplomacy was the wisest course. I excused myself in a little girl voice and made a wide swing around her. Without further mishap I finally managed to set myself down on landing pad one.

Residence Uno was exactly like Crib Deuce, Hacineda Trey or Penthouse Foru: bunks with springs, a small shelf at the foot of each bed, a sink with a metal mirror over it and a commode. In front of the throne stood a tall tin locker, which afforded some toilet privacy if the door was open. There was also a small desk, which served better as a seat.

The bottom bunk was made up, so I went about making the top bunk, obsessed with the idea of getting some sleep. Once I climbed in, Rip Van Winkle's sleeping record was in serious jeopardy of being put to shame. The first problem I encountered was with the mattress cover, which fit my past pallet perfectly but had obviously shrunk up overnight or else my new mattress needed some lessons in weight-watching. After huffing and puffing, stomping on the corners, holding in check a compulsive and overwhelming urge to bite the mother, the mattress was finally encased. When I climbed to the floor again, to view my Herculean accomplishment, all four corners curled up at me in contempt, not to mention the appearance of so many lumps that my gondola looked like a young mountain range. I climbed back onboard, spreadeagled, flapped with both arms and kicked with both heels. The minute I let up pummeling, the darn thing curled right back up. After a few more fruitless bashes, I gave up, forcing myself to look at it optimistically. Hell, if the floods came again, I was equipped with a ready-made boat. Besides that, I doubted if any stray sharks would attack that monstrous looking thing. Who ever heard of a shark leaping at a gondola with a mountain range in the middle anyway?

Both the towel rack and the locker were filled, so all I could do was stack my belongings on the top shelf. The

minute I had everything lined up nice and neat, I tumbled
into the gondola, almost too pooped to pop. A raucous
voice froze my two-second nap.

"Get those things off that shelf!"

She had to be kidding! "You there in the first cell!" She
wasn't.

I crawled to my knees and looked at her through the
bars. It was B.B. and her jibs were so tight I thought for
sure that any minute she'd fire those 90 .mm howitzers at
me.

"There is to be nothing on that shelf except a tin cup and
an ashtray! Do you understand?"

"Well, where do I . . ."

"Are you refusing to obey an order?"

I was still having difficulty adapting to the blind obedience bit, and that continual "do you understand" thing was
getting harder and harder to put up with. For a moment I
envisioned myself down on my haunches, scratching myself
under both arms and jumping up and down like Cheetah in
the Tarzan movies, but commonsense prevailed and I
backed off.

"I understand," I said weakly.

"That's better!" she snapped, unable to resist jamming the
rest of her authoritarian crap down my throat.

She drove away and I took my things down off the shelf,
wondering where the hell I was supposed to put them. Aha!
I could make a pack and strap it to my back. Naw . . .
Maybe I could stuff everything inside my gondola. What
with all the lumps it wouldn't even be noticed. I was still
pondering the problem when intuition told me there was
someone behind me. There was. The trustee, leaning
against the open door. I dangled my legs over the side of
the bunk. Our eyes locked and I felt myself being raped. I
jumped to the floor and stuck my hands self-consciously
into my pockets, checking to make sure her gaze hadn't
seared my dress. She drew deep on a cigarette and smirked
at my nervousness.

"Hi. My name is Ima. What's yours?"

"Norma," she said without emotion. She exhaled slowly and sat on the bottom bunk.

"Please . . . please . . . help me . . ." A disheveled alcoholic stuck her head through the door, obviously in the throes of the D.T.'s. She was ruined and couldn't have looked worse had a tractor-and-trailer hit her and stopped and backed up for a few seconds just to make sure. My stomach gurled with repungance and I had to turn away before it erupted.

Norma wasn't fazed in the least. "Why don't you go find yourself a dime," she said in the same dull voice, "then call somebody who gives a damn. We all got problems, lady."

The wretched woman sagged, hung onto the bars a minute, then somehow found a direction and wobbled away. I was confused at Norma's rudeness and apathy, yet doubted if I would have assisted the woman either—not so much for lack of compassion but because she was so filthy and sick that I couldn't bear the thought of looking at her, let alone touching her. Norma simply wasn't affected in any way.

"Well, where can I put my towel?"

"Move mine over and put it next to that. You can use half the locker for your other things."

I began putting them in the locker, giving each item an extra-loving pat, like a kindly mother who had found some orphans a home and wanted to show them that everything was all right now.

"You ain't plannin' on getting bailed, are you?"

I almost fainted! Some *interest!* At last! I restrained the impulse to go into my old high school "sis-boom-bah" bag. I was eager for some conversation, but at the same time aware of the ways people in jail acted, which was not to display anything. I finished stacking my belongings before I replied.

"I don't know what bail is . . . I haven't been to court yet . . ."

"Nurses line! Nurses line!" The brittle announcement shook the walls, but it turned out to be a blessing in dis-guise, because whoever made the announcement forgot to put the music back on.

"I had a peep at your passport," Norma said. "You got yourself one heavy problem, honey."

I scuffled my feet around. "Yeah, I know . . . See, it wasn't . . ."

"Hold it!" Norma cut in. "I don't give a shit what you did or didn't do. But if you care about yourself, keep your mouth shut about it, else you might find yourself gettin buried alive while some other bitch rolls free at your expense. These walls got ears. You'll be okay if you keep that in mind."

"All late courts line up with your wristbands showing!"

Norma made a face at the loudspeaker. "Shut the fuck up!" She turned her attention back to me. "Don't look like you got much going for yourself at the moment." She took a pack of smokes from the locker. Before she could give me the entire pack I indicated just one cigarette. She laughed that knowing look of hers, busted the pack and gave me one. She x-rayed me again with her eyes and tossed the pack on the bed. "Later, I'll get you whatever else you need."

I couldn't make too much sense out of Norma. One second she came off as a cold, unfeeling individual, and the next she was one of the beautiful people. I liked mucho the second half of her. She handed me a book of matches and I lit up my Pall Mall. It was my first cigarette in some time and the smoke almost choked me.

"Thanks," I coughed, handing her the matches back. She threw the matches next to the cigarettes. "I didn't ask for any of that either, those thank you's." She laughed knowingly again. "Besides, ain't nothing for nothing . . . Remember that, you hear?"

"Ladies! Canteen will be here in half an hour! Have your ditty bags ready!"

Norma flipped her butt into the john. "Got any bread?" I shook my head. "Norma, what are you in here for?"

"Couple robberies and parole violation."

"Parole?" My eyes widened. "You been in prison?"

"Fact is, honey, I been in more than I been out." Her face took on a faraway quality, and I could tell she was reflecting back. For a moment her face softened, but she caught herself quickly and put the barriers back up again. "Lookie here, Ima, I plan to catch me some zzzzzzz's, so you make sure nobody comes in here bothering me. If you want sump'n to occupy your mind there's a mystery novel in the locker." She patted her pillow, while I drooled at how soft it looked. Damn, did I want some sleep!

Norma kicked off her shoes and slid sideways onto her bunk, facing the near wall. "I got a small dress coming in from the other side," she mumbled over her shoulder. "When the trustee runs it this way, get it. Ohh," she added, already half crashed out, "that dress is worth four days in the hole, so be cool . . . and take your cigarettes off my bed."

Norma gave orders in such a confident manner that it never occurred to me to protest. So, wearier than Rip Van Winkle, I found myself face down on my bunk, staring out through the bars, wondering what I was supposed to guard against. Oh well, if a whale swam up, I would just shout "thar she blows!" I giggled at the thought of curling Norma's snuggies with a play like that, but I also kept in mind how she looked when she was angry, so I thought better of the idea. I gave the mystery a few passes before realizing that I had already read it. Besides that my sunken eyeballs were in no shape for a rerun at a tired book. A short time later the trustee came along the outside corridor, whispering Norma's name. I jumped to the floor and went for the dress, which was bundled under her arm. Halfway across the tier I heard my name barked out and almost fainted.

"Ima!"

EEK! Talk about crime prevention! I was caught before I had a chance to do anything wrong!

"Ima Fibbon!" I turned, trying to conceal my fear with a giant *cheeze*. "Take off your underwear and bra and get ready for Blood and V. Hurry!!! I don't have all day!"

When I looked back around again the trustee had disappeared, but I was too confused to be relieved. "What's Blood and V?" I asked another woman walking toward the front.

"Oh, man, they take some blood and check your moneymaker for disease."

I was perplexed about missing the dress pick-up, but more upset at the thought of the forthcoming examination.

"All Blood and V up front!"

A few seconds later twenty of us were crammed into an elevator and speeding toward the top floor. We bounced to a stop.

"Everybody out! All right ladies, no talking! Show your wristbands! Stand single file!" The tight-lipped officer stood stark against the infirmary's sparkling white walls.

Lines of women slowly moved like giant snakes through one door to the next. Everyone appeared mangled and disheveled, yet each managed to maintain enough dignity to avoid the eyes of the other, acutely aware of the upcoming humiliation.

"439126!" I checked my wristband. That was me. "In here!" I stepped into the room, where a doctor immediately closed curtains all around us. "Lay on the table. Put your feet in the stirrups." The thought of what he meant to do caused me to momentarily despise myself for being a woman. I followed his instructions, bracing myself for the alien inspection of my most intimate parts. I wasn't prepared for the excruciating pain that came next. Gawd it hurt! I held my breath while he crudely extracted his utensil, and if it wasn't for the cry I had choked off in my throat, I would have told him that my tonsils could be reached much easier from up top.

"Okay, put your legs together and get up." He flung the curtain back, and as I went out I eyed the next victim with pity. Little did she know that Dr. Jekyll was waiting to turn a painless inspection into a painful one.

Next, I was hustled past a table covered with an array of dixie cups, brimming over with various shades and types of

sugar pills. They probably didn't do much for curing anyone's ills, but they sure looked pretty; a prescription bou-
quet against the pallid walls and ceiling. I didn't have long
to admire the colorful display because I felt myself being
whirled in a circle, the ol' pin-the-tail-on-the-mule, with my
arm turning into the ass. Blood was extracted from me so
fast that I didn't have a chance to yell "ouch." I did check
out the woman who was draining my life's fluid, and I
swear I saw the faint hint of a satisfied smile as she jabbed
my arm. Made me wonder if she was just checking the
blood, or if she had it for dinner with a bacon, lettuce and
tomato sandwich. Either way, she was a whiz with that
spike. Would have made one helluva A-1 dope fiend.

"This way!" Another spin-the-bottle. I turned myself into
a helicopter. After a brief flight around the room I landed
in front of an X-ray machine. "Deep breath! Holdit!"
BOOSH! CLUMP! "Thank you! Next!"

"All ladies who are finished, on the elevator! No talking!"

Who wanted to talk? Who could? The esprit de corps
had been drained out of us, and rag-tagged legionnaires
shuffled toward the elevator, 7th Cavalry returning from
the Little Big Horn, *after* Sitting Bull was finished with
them! As we neared my tier, I foolishly contemplated the
idea of getting off some nod, at last some sleep. Before I
could turn into my driveway a "hey you" stopped me in my
tracks. Stopping was my first mistake. Turning around was
error numeral dugan. A chunky-built woman, with a massive tangle of overly dyed red hair, addressed me.

"You shoppin' canteen today?"

Before I could respond she slapped some money into my
hand. "Good! Stand in line and buy me ten candy bars!" I
hesitated, beginning to understand why Norma never asked.
Nobody asked, they just gave orders. The chunky woman
grew worried at my apparent reluctance and her entire demeanor changed. Her voice was almost a whine.

"I need um bad, baby . . . I'm chuckin', and we can
only get ten apiece . . ."

"Canteen's coming! Everyone in line! No talking! Ditty bags ready!"

"What's a ditty bag?"

"Oh shit! Go get your pillow case! Hurry!" The woman pushed me into a running start. I was back in a mini, huffing and puffing like Wilma Rudolph right after winning the Indianapolis 500 on foot. Even at that I made it only just in time.

"Where's your list?"

"What list?"

"Get out of line!" L.A. C.J.'s finest snapped. "You must have a list!"

I watched the chuck-wagon move out toward the Rockies, without feeding lil' ol' "Priscilla Prickly The Pioneer." Right before it disappeared behind a giant cactus, the red-haired fluff rolled up and unsheathed her verbal tomahawk. I muttered something about a list, while she growled out things like "Dumb assed bitch" and "dizzy broad" and other such delicacies. The situation seemed destined to turn into quite a scene, but it woke Norma up.

"Uh, say, Dinky," she called through the bars at the red-head, "leave Ima alone. She don't know nothin'."

Norma had that right! I gave the woman her money back and dragged myself into the cell. "Did you get the dress?" Norma asked, lighting a cigarette. I had hoped she wouldn't ask. She blew the smoke out in rings, extra slow, so it was easy to see she was holidng in her anger. She exchanged it for some dry sarcasm.

"You didn't get it," she said to herself matter of factly. "Did she come?"

"Yeah, she came." I didn't take any pains to conceal my weariness.

Norma shook her head from side to side. "That broad took a chance on being busted, and you didn't even show up. Boy oh boy . . ."

I was pretty disgusted myself, not only about the dress, but with the entire day. I opened the locker door and plomped down on the commode, trying to decide if I should continue with just the quivering lips or move on up to a cloudburst of tears. An announcement crawled down the tier.

"Ladies! Get ready! A tour is coming."

Norma giggled, obviously no longer upset about the dress, came over and slapped me on the knee. "C'mon, Ima, suck it back in. You don't want them peeps viewing you on the throne, do you?"

What a trip! What a place! Not even enough peace for a girl to sit down and have a simple cry.

At last! Sleep! I just let everything go and sank into my long awaited slumber. Hmm . . . did it feel good! Eventually, my journey into the land of zzzz's was invaded by a dream, a brilliant light shining from on high, accompanied by a dreamy voice that kept crooning my name.

"Ima! Ima! IMA!"

Oh no! It wasn't no dream! I blinked my beepers open and sho'nuf, there was the friendly neighborhood policeman, pointing her flashlight at me face.

"Hurry up! Get dressed! You're going to court!"

Court? The sun wasn't even up yet. Eyes still plastered together with the sandman's refuse, I eased off the bed, careful lest the squeaking wake Norma. When my feet touched the icy cement, I stifled a gasp, not only because of the sharp chill on my moon men, but because my nightgown had caught on a loose spring. My predicament was such that I had to remain poised on my toes or risk tearing my nightgown. In a state of near-panic, I counted to ten, then again, and once more for good measure, then forced myself to be calm while I figured out the alternatives: I could stand there the rest of my life, try the risky business of climbing back up and untangling the gown, or I could just say "fuck it", rip the mother loose and put up with Norma's growling.

Norma made my decision for me. She startled me with her whisper. "You going to court?"

"Yeah", I said, raising up on tip-toes. If I could make the

Othello Noel

gown slack, a quick jerk might tear it free with little damage. I jerked hard. Instead of the loud, tearing noise which usually accompanied cloth ripping, my yank encountered no resistance at all. In fact, I must have freed the gown entirely, because I tumbled into the locker, causing a skelter of noise and banging bones on metal. I thought sure, at the very least, my elbow was broken. My funny bone sent a charge up my arm that brought tears to my eyes.

"Ima! What the hell you doin'?" Norma hissed.

"My gown was caught!" I hissed right back at her. My crazy bone was raising havoc with my arm and I was in no mood for anyone hassling me.

Norma laughed and lit a cigarette. The glow made her face visible and I could see her propped up on an elbow. "Don't worry. This is just for a plea. They'll tell you to say you ain't guilty and to come back in two weeks."

"What? . . . Oh yeah . . ." I was too busy primping in the dark to pay full attention to what Norma was saying.

"You got any peeps out there, Ima?"

"Hmm hmm," I gurgled with my toothbrush jammed in my jibs," mby mbolks, mband ma mbew mbriends . . . Mbhy?"

"Because you'll be able to use a telephone, that's why." She fumbled around in her pillow-case. "Here, here's a dime. Make sure you call collect, so you can use it over again. Don't lend it to nobody, you understand, rubberband? That goes for smokes too!" She motioned toward the locker. "Take a pack, but keep in mind that that stuff comes hard in here, so don't go playin' the role of some good time samaritan with the goodies. These moochin' bitches will drain you dry. You dig?"

Gurgle, gurgle, gurgle, bwoosh! "Gee, thanks". Norma viewed my "gee's" and "gollies" with much distaste, because to her these were expressions of naivety and an open invitation to the jailhouse hustlers and con artists. Yet lifelong training and habits are not easy things to discard, and I was having very little success with the ejection of the Ima Fibbon I had known all my life.

"Duh, shucks, ma'am," Norma mimicked. With a chuckle, she pulled the covers up to her chin and rolled over.

My head spun. Where was my dress? How was I supposed to comb my hair in the dark? How was I expected to make a good impression in front of the judge? It was bad enough just going in front of one, because already I was in possession of a long-seeded image of those stern-faced individuals. enshrouded in their black robes, scowling down at the fallen from their heaven-high benches. It gave me the shivers to think of myself in the clutches of these self-proclaimed gods, so I conjured up Perry Mason for the defense. After a few magic exchanges with "his honor," Perry smiled benevolently and said, "justice has been served, Ima. Go in peace."

I was still drooling at myself—walking arm in arm with those I loved, out of the courtroom and into the sun—when reality struck.

"All courts stand back! When your door opens, step out and come to the front immediately!"

"Bye, baby." Norma's tone was warm and gentle, and I tried to see her face in the gloom. I couldn't, because of the semi-darkness and because she had turned toward the wall again. Her hair was braided and this somehow indicated the mellow Norma, the woman behind the tough facade. "Don't worry 'bout your bed. I'll make it up."

The doors rattled open. Myself and several other courts lined up at the tier gate. I glanced at a wall clock. It was four in the morning. After surveying my court pals, however, I didn't feel half as bad about my appearance, because any one of us could have easily won the "Miss Nightmare" title, going away.

Our first stop was the mess hall. The dimly-lit hallway was so cold that my teeth began to chatter. As I took my tray from the rack, my heart warmed at the thought of digging into some hot grub, until, that is, I saw that the main course was SOS, initials for a concoction commonly referred to by residents as "shit on the shingle." A woman behind me started humming under her breath: "If it was good enough for my army daddy, it's good enough for me."

I probably would have been amused, were I not so hungry and had the time been appropiate for human life, rather than hours before the chickens started scratching. But at least the coffee was hot, and while I sipped I noticed that one woman was actually shoveling in the main dish. I caught her attention, motioned with my spoon to my SOS, then her coffee. She nodded and we made the exchange I felt really proud of myself, my first transaction without the assistance of Norma's eyes there to clue me in. The only thing lacking for my moment of triumph was the New York Philharmonic, playing their rendition of the Notre Dame Victory March as a tribute to my craftiness in jailhouse bargaining.

"All courts file out! Deposit your spoons at the door!"

We marched through an acre of hallways and into the booking area, where we waited in a crammed, smokey room. A few minutes later we were called one by one and ushered into another room. This was filled with a row of dressing stalls.

"439126!"

I jumped forward, immediately cursing myself for so quickly responding to a number, automatically. The action fightened me, not only because my name had been exchanged for a number in a file, but because in my own mind I was beginning to lose sight of my true identity. The habitual finger pointed directions.

Inside still another room, a trustee in a striped dress handed me my street clothes from an alcove with a Dutch door. I had completely forgotten my navy blue bells, blue workshirt and sandals. I slipped into them as quickly as possible, even though no one gave the "hurry up" order. Once again I reprimanded myself for the conditioning that was taking place within me.

After I dressed I sat waiting, until I saw another woman march to the closet and turn in her jail clothes. I emulated her, now acutely aware of my lack of individual identity, but

finding it much easier to fall in with the regimented procedure.

In wrinkled civvy splendor, we were marched from the
building and into the back of a bus, where an officer
checked our wristbands before marking off our numbers on
a clipboard.

It was pitch black outside and my attempt to get a
glimpse of the sky was in vain. The summer sun was the
only thing that could penetrate the light fog, and it had not
stuck its smiling face over the horizon yet.

I found myself a seat by a window, looking forward to
the ride. I felt a deep tiny tingle when the big engine roared
to life and we pulled out into the street. Eagerly, I peered
out the window, wondering if freedom was still free, if people walked the streets and children still galloped around
like crazy while shopping with their mothers. All I could
see in the gloom was desertion—desolate gray streets and
sidewalks, dotted on occasion by a sparse patch of green, or
a tree. After a while I just stared out, but at nothing, merely pointing my eyes.

We stopped at another jail, the men's hotel, and there we
ended up in a holding tank, with six benches bolted to the
walls and a telephone booth. On one side of the tank an officer sat enclosed in a thick glass cage. I fought down the
urge to shout "will the real goldfish please stand up?" There
was no sink or any other toilet facilities, so I gathered that
mother nature wasn't allowed to function, unless she got
busted.

My first thought was the telephone, but after watching the
swarm of screaming and clawing women there, I decided it
was best to wait. I lit a cigarette and occupied myself by
admiring the artwork on the walls of the penal museum.
Most of the graffiti was from one human to another, tatoos
of devotion: "Baby loves Peaches. Bobby and Sue por
vida." A few slogans expressed other ideas: "Viva la Raza!
Jesus saves! God is alive and well—he's hiding in Argen-
tina!"

The clamor around the telephone reached nerve-wracking proportions, and a craving for solitude overtook me. The thick smoke in the air also began to affect me, so I crushed out my cigarette and found myself a seat on the floor.

An hour later, an officer called numbers over an intercom. We lined up at the door, showed our wristbands, then boarded the bus as our numbers were called relentlessly.

"439126." I climbed onboard.

This time there were men sitting in the rear. I had been on buses before with men, but under far different circumstances, and never gazing through a wire-mesh, or listening to the Tarzan/Jane wolf-whistles, all in tune with the rattling of chains and shackles. I settled in for an interesting ride.

"Anyone looking back will be written up and taken immediately to lock-up upon our return!"

We booed the villian, but turned to face forward, pouting. The majority dreaded lock-up, much more than a hurried love affair through a screen, yet a few continued to play, finding that the insinuating smiles and eye signals were worth the risk.

By the time our chariot backed into the courthouse unloading area, the sun had turned the sky into a rainbow of smoggy colors.

"Ladies first".

An elevator zipped us to the top. Four right turns, three lefts, one dip and a curve later, we were deposited into still another holding tank. It was a duplicate of the last tank, but in miniature. Neither was there a glass cage or an officer present, so two women took advantage of the situation and set up house. I looked away quickly as they embraced and exchanged a yard of tongue. I wasn't repulsed, but rather frightened at the unfamiliarity of the scene. I concentrated on the walls, nearly bored with the incarcerated jottings—until, that is, I spotted Norma's name on the makeshift billboard. I gasped at the thought of my bunkie being a lesbian, then asked myself if it really mattered. I finally decided that she was my friend and that that was all I'd need to go on.

A hand on my shoulder scared the nibbles out of me. It was the same woman who'd been behind me in the mess hall. She was a small, pretty blonde. She ran her fingers through her short-cropped hair and pointed at Norma's name.

"That's your tight, ain't it?"

Innocently, I asked of whom she was speaking.

"Whom!" she exclaimed with a laugh. "You know damn well, whom!" She laughed again and emphasized, "whom else?"

"Well . . . You could have meant someone else." I blushed, realizing my own susceptibility.

She motioned to the other name with her cigarette. "Don't worry, that other broad is long gone."

"You don't understand. We're only . . ." I knew my face was beet red.

Her blue eyes twinkled. "Have no fear, sweetie, you're safe with me." She pulled a pack of cigarettes from her blouse pocket and offered me one. I showed her mine, but she insisted on giving me one anyway. Before I could find my matches she was ready with a light. James Dean should've been so cool!

"Thank you." I spoke coyly, then excused myself from her penetrating eyes by heading for the telephone.

After six attempts to call someone I gave up. Every number I tried came up blank, but at least I still had my dime. I tucked it back in my bra and started toward a different seat. The blonde caught my attention and patted the bench next to her. I felt obligated, since I had accepted that damn cigarette, so I guessed that made us friends of sorts. The thought of another woman making me ill-at-ease was confusing and discomforting, but I swallowed the lump in my throat and forced a grin.

"What's your name?" I asked her.

"Sparky . . . and yours is Ima."

A few minutes later I found myself involved in the game

Othello Noel

of "how did you know?" Every word seemed to fit into a performance, part of which included an obvious pleasure at my uneasiness. I reached for one of my own cigarettes, but before I had it shook loose, Sparky had the match lit.

"You're just a baby," she said soothingly, "and you're doing right by sticking with Norma. Just don't ever do her wrong though, you hear? Of course, if you ever do . . . Well, let's just say you got a friend in me." She winked. "Count on that, okay?"

There was no way to respond to that, so I changed the subject. "What do you do?"

Sparky laughed. "Time." I caught onto her humor and laughed myself.

"So, you'll be in for a while, eh?" Now Sparky was probing and I wasn't having any double-standards, plus I remembered what Norma had told me: "No one is to be trusted!"

"I really don't know what's going to happen."

"Well, lookie here . . . If you come to the joint, I'll make sure you get off on the right foot."

A commitment was being offered and I wanted no part of it. Once again, Sparky had succeeded in making me nervous. "Well, I don't really know what's gonna happen."

Sparky raised an eyebrow and peered at me. "Think about it."

At about 10 o'clock, a female bailiff called my name. We traveled 'round the bend, past the end, by pack train through the Sierra Madres, finally arriving in the courtroom. The only sound there was the rustle of clothing from the waiting audience. I was parked in front of the judge's bench, where a male bailiff asked me if my baptismal handle was Ima Fibbon.

"Affirmative."

The judge appeared indifferent, and in that genre questioned me about whether or not I had an attorney.

"Negative."

Next thing I knew, a tall, slender man, wearing a gray

suit and a peppermint tie, slid out of the wallpaper. He mumbled nervously in my ear and handed me a card.

"I'll be up to see you as soon as I can. Plead not guilty."

"Ima Fibbon," His Honor queried, "how do you plead?"

I twisted my hands behind my back. "Not guilty." I held my breath, almost expecting some sort of hue and cry from the spectators, something like "off with her head!" But there was not a word, only the heavy feel of goggling eyes as they pierced my back.

"Very well," the judge sighed. "I direct your case to courtroom one oh nine, where a preliminary hearing will be held in two weeks."

"Is that all there is?" I asked my female escort.

"That's it. Walk faster, please. I have a long list of cases and I want to finish before lunch."

When I returned to the tank, I noted that Sparky was engrossed in a conversation. The woman she rapped with looked like a case of plastic surgery that had failed. Sparky picked me up the minute I entered and signaled for me to sit next to her. As soon as I sat down she put her hand on my knee. The gesture made me uneasy, but I didn't pull away. Sparky winked at me knowingly, realizing that I wasn't going to object, because on the surface the act was quite innocent. She continued her conversation with the other woman.

"Man, that's a tough break." Sparky shook her head from side to side. "Are you going to try for the joint, maybe get out of the program?"

"I don't know . . . Is there any choice?" The woman reached to straighten her knotted hair, found a hairpin and stuck it between her teeth. She had some job in front of her and I didn't think MGM's hairdresser could straighten out that mess. "Five years of naline," she gritted. "You know they must be tired of my ass by now." She popped the pin in another spot, but just as I suspected, her hair looked the same, except maybe for a reverse angle.

Sparky went on with the investigation. It was difficult to

tell whether she was sincerely interested or just being nosey. "So, how'd you get shot down?"

"Aw, man, you wouldn't believe it." Sparky gave her a cigarette, which served as encouragement. "I was doin' this burglary, dig?" Sparky and I nodded while she exhaled some smoke. "And everything was going super cool, not a creature was stirrin', not even a mouse . . ." She paused to giggle at her own witticism. "And when I left, my arms was full of goodies. It was a beautiful score and a clean getaway. That was when I got greedy, like there was so much I left behind, ya know?" She spread her arms, like in the giant fish story. "On the third trip, the fuzz met me comin' out the door. I couldn't figure it, 'cause *nobody*, and I mean *nobody*, was anywhere in sight! Well, I ask one of these cops how they got a why on me, and one dude points up to the sky. Well, who should be there but this goddamn telephone repairman! Not only that, but the son-of-a-bitch has the nerve to wave good-bye to me!" Her face mirrored her disbelief. "Now, ain't that about a bitch?"

"You're shittin' me!" Sparky exclaimed.

"Naw, man, that's square biz. But I can dig where you're comin' from. I can hardly believe the shit myself."

I began to feel like part of the conversation and inched in closer. Sparky took her hand off my knee and introduced us. "Dee Dee . . . Ima. Ima . . . Dee Dee."

Not especially enthused at the new acquaintance, Dee Dee half nodded at my big smile. "This is Ima's first fall," Sparky said. Dee Dee's features softened.

"What's naline?" I wanted to know.

"A jive test for dope fiends, baby, and it's a bitch."

"Oh, you mean a test for . . .?" I sounded naive and knew it.

"That's right, honey . . . hmm hmm hmm . . . Wish I could get a positive right now." Her eyes shut and peace came over her face, just at the thought of a heroin high.

I was fascinated. "I've never shot any of that stuff. What does it do?"

"It makes the world go away," Dee Dee dreamed, "just the way the guy asks for in the song."

"So, what's gonna happen now?" Sparky asked.

Dee scratched her cheek. "Man, I dunno." Suddenly she popped her fingers and stared at me. "Hey! Now I know you! You been walkin' with Norma, right?"

Sparky answered for me. "Yeah, that's her roomie." I was glad in a way that she had spoken in my place, because even though she had been playing with my awkwardness, I wasn't about to let the whole damn jail give me a hard time.

Sparky swung the conversation around. "What happened in court, Ima?"

"Oh, nothin' . . ."

Sparky curled her upper lip. "Nothin' ever does. You see, we ain't zero to these mothers, just numbers in a jive numbers game." She kicked at a butt that was on the floor.

"Well, I'll tell you one thing for sure," Dee Dee put in, "I'm gettin' off the merry-go-round this time."

"Is that so?" Sparky took no pains to hide her cynicism.

"Yeah, man, I been in this amusement park too long, and I'm bailing out now." Dee Dee began to shiver, even though it wasn't cold.

"I hope you make it," I told Dee, not feeling that it was fair for Sparky to knock her good intentions.

The conversation rolled on and on, for what seemed like a month. When an officer strolled into the tank, two decades later, our rumps were sore and our smokes were on empty. She called our numbers and lined us up. At last! Home sweet home! I caught myself. What home? Oh well, at least Norma was there, but then again, I had come to like Sparky too.

The men were on the bus already, but most of us were too burnt out to play peek-a-boo. To my dismay, a few minutes later we turned into the parking lot of the first holding tank.

"Now ain't that a bitch!" Sparky growled.

"Ain't it?" I echoed.

"Aw shit!" a woman in the back snapped, as another bus passed us going out. "That means we ain't going back till this fuckin' place fills up again, and that could be hours!"

Our chariot squeaked to a halt. "All right ladies . . . out."

The tank was twice as dirty the second time around, and by now everyone was dog tired, with nerves sho 'nuf frazzled. In the space of ten minutes, two fights started and were broken up. I listened with half an ear while another pair bickered as to whom their pimp would bail out first. It would be interesting to see which one would be missing from the mess line. My bet was the shorter of the two, mostly because I felt the taller hustler exaggerated the amount of money she brought home to daddy. There were some mental cases in with us too, but the other women bombed them with an array of optical threats, like "don't you dare go off now!" Most of these women sat alone, mumbling to themselves. Several women cried, while still others held hands, saddened by the fact that their new found loves would soon be gone forever. All in all, we were a sorry bunch, and I couldn't help thinking about and agreeing with the various articles I'd read, concerning what prisons did to the human mind. It caused me to dwell on a passage from a poem titled, The Ballad Of Reading Gaol, which had been written by Oscar Wilde:

> I walked, with other souls in pain,
>   Within another ring,
> And was wondering if the man had done
>   A great or little thing,
> When a voice behind me whispered low,
>   "That fellow's got to swing.

Finally a bus arrived and took us back to the County Jail. We went through the checking out procedures, but in reverse. We showed our wristbands and were escorted to our tiers. On my way by, I spotted Norma in the T.V. room. She was concentrating heavily on a game of Tonk with Rio, her partner from the streets. She didn't see me

Othello Noel

and I was too tired to get her attention. I shuffled into the cell, plopped down on the desk and began massaging my weary dogs. I was sho 'nuf ready for some R&R!

"All late dinners from court, to the dining area! All late dinners . . ."

The cell gate opened and, what the hell, people in jail are always hungry. The mess hall was half full. On the way to my seat I passed Sparky. Dee Dee occupied a seat next to her, not eating, but simply staring at the floor. Sparky gobbled down her own food, switched trays with Dee, and then scoffed up her portion too. When my tank number was called, I picked up my tray and spoon, brushing Sparky's back on my way by.

I dragged into my cell, engulfed again with visions of slumber. It was well past lights-out and all were tucked in for the night. Norma was still awake.

"Hi there." She'd been reading a magazine, using the light that filtered through the bars from the outside catwalk. She seemed happy to have me back.

I took off my dress and wriggled into my gown, wondering where to begin. "There were so many things . . . I didn't get anyone on the phone . . . I met Sparky and a friend of hers, Dee Dee . . . She's gonna kick her habit and . . ."

"Hold it baby." Norma smiled tenderly. "Slow down before you get flagged for speeding. You look tired, so you can tell me in the morning, okay?"

"That sounds cool." I tossed my dress into the locker, noting that I was beginning to feel comfortable with Norma. I hopped up onto my bunk, then leaned over the edge.

"Goodnight."

Norma reached up and tossled my hanging hair. I started to touch one of her braids, but hesitated. She tossled my hair again.

"Go ahead."

"I can?" I asked shyly.

She smiled. "Sure, baby."

I twisted a braid around my finger. I felt good about Norma, really solid, and lucky that I had found a rosebud in the manure pile. I closed my eyes and went to sleep, with that thought in my head.

Norma and I went to church on Sunday. We had two purposes for attending: it offered a chance for fresh air, as the chapel was located outside, and we wanted to see Sparky. We weren't interested in threats of God's wrath, which was always the weekly sermon, and on this occasion I almost interrupted the speaker to ask if he had a hot line from above. He sure sounded like he was in direct contact.

Five minutes after the service started, one woman began feeling the spirit and started shouting. "Hallelujah! Praise the Lord!" Heads turned toward the back, where an elderly woman, with skinny arms and wearing a shrunk-up sweater, had stood up and was waving her arms in the air. "Thank you, Jesus!" she ranted, with tears in her eyes. Several police, who had been patrolling the aisle, closed in on the woman. She was grabbed under the armpits and escorted out. Amen!

The pianist struck a few chords and we stood in unison to the speaker's all-encompassing hand-sweep, then listened to the opening refrain of "The Old Rugged Cross."

"Where are they . . . taking her?" I sang in tune with the music.

"To the old . . . M.O. ward", Norma sang back, "where they keep . . . all the nuts . . ."

Across the way I spotted Sparky and Dee Dee and smiled a hello. When the song ended we sat down. Sparky's small hands moved in gestures, which Norma had to interpret for me. My roomie caught Dee Dee's attention and rubbed her arm, indicative of asking her if she wanted some dope. Norma made sure I was watching. Dee Dee nodded emphatically.

"Fool ass woman!" Norma whispered. "She ain't giving up shit, just the words sound pretty."

Sparky caught up with us on the way out. Her blue eyes were red and it was obvious she was under the influence of something beside the atmosphere. She asked if we wanted to get bombed out, speaking openly and without bothering to put any shade on herself. The idea of dope inside the jail made me nervous and I shook my head. I didn't want any part of it.

"Beatrice! What are you doing out of line?" The livid-lipped officer stood right next to us. "Let me see your wrist-bands!" We did and she jotted all three of our numbers. "You are not to return to church for three weeks!"

Hallelujah! Sure wasn't no big thing with me, because I had no plans on coming back in three years. The only thing I learned was Sparky's name, which made it understandable why she had adopted the Sparky monicker. Beatrice? Yuk!

"We sure blew that, huh?" I whispered to Norma.

"You mean church?" Norma seemed quite unaffected by the whole affair, and more interested in getting into the cell. "Hey! Officer! Open cell one!" The door grumbled open and we sauntered in.

"Once a month is more than enough religion for me," Norma scoffed. She slapped my back and laughed at her reflection in the mirror.

"You got that right." I lit a smoke. "How long you guys been doing this?"

"Oh . . . about as long as long is," Norma responded offhandedly. She ta te da'd a bit and patted her afro. "How come you wanted to go see Sparky?" She turned around and teased me with a smile.

"Line up in two's and proceed to the dining area!" the box barked, before I had a chance to answer.

We leaped out, because whoever was swinging the doors must have thought she had a bunch of Flash Gordon's under her command, and the second the sliding gates banged open, they were grinding closed again.

The tier was full of unruly women, dancing and giggling at each other. It was evident that half the tank was zonked out. The procession to the mess hall was a straggly one, and when Norma had trouble making it up a ramp, I knew she was high as a buzzard in heat. I guessed she had gotten something from Sparky, even though I hadn't seen the action, but flying my roomie was, and without wings.

When we got to the mess hall we found a woman lying in the doorway, face down. I stopped.

"Step around! Keep the line moving! I said—STEP AROUND!"

Like zombies marching through limbo, we all silently obeyed. The woman just lay there on the floor, while someone went to get a wheel chair. From what I'd heard about the infirmary, she was probably better off right where she was.

As it was normally, just sitting on the little mess-hall stools was a risky proposition, but that day most of the women found it near impossible. A resident next to me plopped off hard, then wobbled up cursing like a muleskinner. Another woman collapsed in the meal line and telephones started buzzing. When still another woman went down for the count and a little red pill rolled out of her pocket, the stuff was on! An officer nearby picked up the pill, gasped and ran to a wall alarm. Beepers beeped, bells banged, horns honked, and it sounded like one of those SAC Red-Alerts. Brass stormed quickly into the mess hall, like a swarm of bees hot on the case of a honey-looting bear; sergants, lieutenants, captains and a couple generalissmos for good measure. I watched in awe.

Lines were pulled out of the mess hall—it was well before the alloted fifteen minutes—and we were pushed into the T.V. room instead of our tank.

"How come they put us here?" I asked Norma.

She was hot. "What the fuck you think we're here for? They're searching for the reds!" I started to say something else, but she cut me off. "I don't wanna hear it!"

A short time late the uniformed search-party moved into our tank. We watched intently through a window in the door as the searchers went on a binge, reminiscent of a bunch of ol' biddy's let loose at a bargain basement sale. Things were thrown every which way, boxes were turned over, linen was tossed onto the floor, ashtrays were dumped indiscriminately. Everything not bolted down received the business, and not even the pictures on the walls were spared. One officer found a smoking kite in Rio's cell, and squealed her delight. Others gathered around, while the guard read it aloud. We could hear what was being said clearly in the T.V. room. Rio stood alone in a corner, pink with embarrassment and rage.

Most of the women in the T.V. room involved themselves with hasty attempts at sobering up. Some primped, some did exercises, while a few practiced walking a straight line. We would all be scrutinized closely, and a clumsy move could lead to a urine test, which always revealed if there were drugs in the system or not. I eyed Norma from time to time, but she remained cool and as far as I could tell, was in complete control of her head. We didn't have any worries as far as contraband was concerned, because I hadn't collected any and Norma always made her stash outside the cell.

For a while it appeared as if our tank was going to get away clean. It was my thought that maybe everything had been consumed. At about that point a sergeant struck gold. She came out onto the freeway, carrying a pillowcase. She set it down and began pulling pills from it by the fistfull. Her expression was one of crazed joy. This discovery would garner her plenty of extra points, and could even lead to a promotion.

Two hours went by before we were allowed back into the tier. As we walked from the T.V. to the tank, any woman walking wobble-legged was pulled out of line for a urine test. I could barely conceal my relief when Norma and I passed through unmolested.

Our cell reflected a disaster area, after a heavy romance with a tornado, and as we stood open-mouthed, wondering where to start cleaning up at, B.B. decided to make a patrol along the catwalk.

"Ladies! Your cells are a mess!" she piped. "Double scrub! There will be an inspection shortly!"

Rio's cell had been hit the hardest, though it was not the

one which had given up the Big Red bust. "Officer! Can I have some clean linen? My sheets are full of ashes."

"Linen is distributed only on Wednesdays," B.B. informed Rio distantly, then was gone with a ring of her keys.

Rio rolled her eyes at the ceiling. She stood with hands on hips, her lips tight, and her eyes filled with suppressed rage. "That motherfucker!" she growled low in her throat. "That low-lifed, robot-assed *bitch!* Oooooh!"

Three weeks later I received my first visit. The visiting room was a shoddy affair, with sectioned-off aisles and stools, similiar to those in the mess hall. In front of each stool was a thick glass window, and a telphone for communication. The visiting room officer pushed two one-dollar bills at me, then slid a receipt pad and a dulled pencil stub across the desk.

"Sign here." I did. "Window thirteen."

As it was a weekday, the room was fairly empty. Most people came on weekends, due to working schedules. My visitor was Julie, a friend from the old neighborhood. Her bright colorful clothing and neatly curled hair appeared foreign to me. A pimp in the next seat ogled her, obviously interested in her possibilities. The more he stared, the more Julie squirmed, and there was a mixture of excitement and fear on her sheltered face. She had trouble starting the conversation, so I began firing questions on the telephone, about the friends we knew and the places where we used to hang out. This eased the tension somewhat, and soon we were gossiping like a pair of freshly unmuzzled magpies.

Our twenty minutes ended in five seconds, much too fast, and in the middle of thanking Julie for the two dollars the receiver was cut off. At first I thought the phone might have gone on the blink, but after I shook it till it rattled, I realized the phone was all right. It had been killed by a human and there was no question of resurrection. I waved goodbye to Julie and carefully formed the words "come

again." She blew me a kiss and nodded. After that she showed every week.

Norma was pleased to see that I had some money. New
bookings came into the tank regularly, and since they never
brought cigarettes or candy, those with money were more
than willing to pay extra for items. By stocking heavy, Norma and I could increase our income rather handsomely, by
selling the victuals for double the price. Of course, since
there was a limit as to how many cigarettes and candy bars
each resident could purchase at one time, we preferred payment in supplies rather than case. This way, we managed to
constantly stock-up, but without spending any of our own
money. Naturally, such a practice was frowned upon by the
authorities, but what the shucks, some of those people
frowned on breathing.

"Just don't feel sorry for anyone," Norma schooled.
"Most of these folks will split before you do anyway. If
they complain about the price, don't worry about it, because there's always another train on the same track. Besides, we got the only store on the tier, so it's either us or
wait. You dig? Another game you got to watch for is somebody sayin' you ought to give 'em a break, because they're
my friend. Don't go for that, as my tights all know that this
is my hustle, know what I mean, jellybean?"

I enjoyed the excitement of becoming Norma's business
partner. "I understand, rubberband."

Our next canteen was that night and after we made our
purchases, Norma dumped the diddy bags on the bed. She
rubbed her hands briskly together.

"Okay! Let's check out the goodies!"

Our store turned out to be a huge success and it brought
enough profit to easily support one of my newly acquired
pleasures—gambling. I found it to be a relaxing pastime.
Of course I was no Cincinnati Kid at Tonk, Bid Wisk or
Poker, but Norma more than made up for what I dropped,
as she rarely lost.

The yuletide approached. This was always a depressing
period for women in jail, as thoughts turned to families,

children and friends. There would be no chestnuts roasting on any open fires, nor would Saint Nick be wise if he fooled around in the bleak confines of C.J., unless he wanted to find himself posing for a mug shot.

'Twas the night before Christmas when Sparky sent me a note, with a tab of acid enclosed. I split the tablet with Norma, and we tripped throughout the night. The usually nerve-wracking sounds of women snoring became a hilarious experience. Later, I just stared at the walls and ceiling, which became a lacework of soft, intricately patterned women's faces.

At breakfast I looked for Sparky, but she wasn't in the mess hall. Dee Dee caught my questioning look and signaled that she was in the hole. I spent the rest of the meal thinking about Sparky. Finally, I decided that I would join her in lock-up

"Damn her!" I said to Norma, back on the tier. "Why on Christmas?"

"Whatcha gonna do about it?" Norma baited.

"Go down there and wish her a Merry Christmas," I retorted.

Norma popped her fingers gleefully and went through some Flip Wilson motions.

"Only one thing, Norma . . . what if they . . ."

"That's a possibility." Norma had the same thought, that perhaps we might be separated. The rule was "you move, you lose," and if a new booking showed and you were in the hole, welp, you could find your things out on the doorstep when you showed back.

Norma squinted at me. "Ahhhh . . . . I might be able to maintain the fort, so I'll hold onto your stuff, okay?" She touched my cheek with the back of her hand and smiled. "You go ahead and wish Miss Mean a Merry Christmas, and give her hell for being down there." She moved toward the bed. "As for me, I'm after a heap of zzzz's. That acid is wearing off and I'm one weary sucker."

I strolled to the front of the tier and asked B.B. if she would kindly sharpen my pencil.

"You'll have to wait! I'm busy!"

That was the usual answer and the one I'd been waiting for. It gave me an excuse to start spouting out foul language and I told her in layman's terms what I thought of her and her jail. She wasn't too busy after that little barrage and before I could say "plinkety plunk" I found myself in the empty T.V. room. A few minutes later, the sergeant who'd busted open the Red Connection showed up. We had encountered each other on previous occasions, (although those were relatively mild meetings) so we weren't strangers.

"Ima? What is this?" The sergeant's tone was brittle.

I waved my arms in disgust. "I'm tired! I've had it! I just don't care anymore!"

"Ima, now you just simmer down." I almost fainted! Where was Sergeant Regulations coming from, actually trying to soothe me? "When in Rome, it is wise to do as the Romans do." She beamed at her own philosophic plagiarism.

"Never!" I felt silly at my dramatics, but some of the acid was still in my system, and it bolstered my devil-may-care attitude. "Just because I love pizza, doesn't mean I have to act as a Roman! I refuse!" I fixed her with my Henrietta VIII glare, thinking, "eat your heart out, Richard Burton, 'cause Ima Fibbon is a natural."

The sergeant continued trying to reason with me. "It's Christmas, and I don't want to bring you punishment on this holy day. In fact, I'm going to overlook your actions, in the hope that you will repay my kindness by behaving yourself in the future."

I didn't really want a vendetta with the sergeant, so I backed up. "Okay," I muttered, and slouched all the way back to my tank.

B.B. let me in, seemingly unaffected, except that her jaws were so tight, her cheeks were twitching.

I entered our cell like a whupped dog with his tail tucked between his legs. Just my luck! On the day I was loaded for bear, everyone else was practising humanity. Norma was still in the bed, but propped on her elbow smoking.

"What happened, baby?" She looked confused, since the whole tier had heard first hand the "sharpened pencil affair", and that was supposed to be some sho 'nuf long gone lock-up.

"Aw man . . ." I mumbled. "Everybody's full of good will, favors, all that shit."

Norma handed me a cigarette, trying to hold back the laughter. She dropped the smoke on the floor and we both doubled up in delirium. Soon, we were screeching until the tears ran from our eyes.

Before mess I got another brainstorm. Norma giggled at what I planned to do, but expressed some doubts about whether or not I would follow through. I lit my cigarette and sat on the table, feeling it as my adrenalin began to build in anticipation of the upcoming "Ima Fibbon Christmas Special."

We entered the mess hall in the usual manner. Norma was behind me, but quiet, just observing. Wide-eyed I looked around, completely discarding the "Cagney" shade.

"Eyes straight ahead!"

I took a deep breath, then shouted at the top of my lungs, "Merry Christmas!"

Everything stopped dead, but I noticed that most of the long faces had changed into grins. Thus encouraged, I began hollering to everyone I knew, then to some peeps I didn't know. Each of them responded with a "Merry Christmas" and a smile. Finally, the yuletide spirit was strangled by prison discipline, in the form of two officers who pulled me out of line.

They hustled me off to a different T.V. room. This was closer to the mess hall. Women passing by asked if I was all right or not, and one woman rolled a lit cigarette under the door. Ten minutes later they came for me. Two women and a male waded through the smoke from my recently clinched cigarette. I grinned sheepishly.

"Ima! Come with us!"

I was hoping one of them would smile. After all, I hadn't stolen the Pentagon Papers! "Where am I going?"

"Just come along!"

I gulped. Their somber expressions made me feel like I was headed for the last mile.

We went through hallways, down ramps—always down. The deeper we got the quieter it became. Eventually, we reached a level where there was no music. Instead, the tank echoed with a variety of sounds.

"Hey! Officer! If you don't give me a cigarette, God is gonna send you to hell!" Another voice spewed out every swear word in existence. When she ran out of those, she invented some of her own. Vocal chords were at full strength.

"Shut those goddamn nuts up!" This came from the other side of the tank. I was escorted to that side.

"So, this is lock-up?" I was hoping someone would say, "yup, now you know, so you can go back upstairs." Instead, I was frisked bare.

The tier gate opened. "Cell ten!"

The freezing faces hadn't melted one degree. I walked by the cells, afraid to look in on the inhabitants.

"Hey! Ima!" It was Rio.

I stopped. "Rio! What are you still doing down here?" She had disappeared the day after the "Reds Bust".

"Move on, Ima!" I took another look at Norma's disheveled partner and scurried away.

"Izzat you, Ima?" a familiar voice queried, shouting over the other noises.

The atomosphere was eerie and tense, but I tried to make light of my fear. "Yeah, it's me . . . Zat you?"

Sparky laughed. I figured she was about five cells away, toward the back, and I fought against the urge to run past cell ten to see her.

"You know it is, girl. How come you're here?" I couldn't imagine why Sparky sounded in such good spirits. I was ready to go back upstairs.

"Figgered I'd come down and wish ya'll a Merry Christmas." My voice was beginning to crack.

"Hey! Rio! Did you hear?"

"Yeah," Rio bellowed.

"That's my baby," Sparky concluded with a little squeal. I looked over my shoulder, still tempted to run and see

Sparky, but the male officer was starting down the tier menacingly.

"I said . . . Get into cell ten . . . NOW!"

I ran inside, and after the door slammed behind me, I stood in the center of the cell, until my eyes adjusted to the gloom. There were Corn Flakes glued to the wall, most of the springs were missing from the bed, and there was no locker. Lipstick writings were everywhere, floor, ceiling, walls, and the most interesting notice referred to a former king of rock and roll: "Elvis Presley is my wife."—He is, huh? Well, I'd like to inform you, your old lady is dead. She died from a heart attack, after a hound dog shit on his blue suede shoes."

Someone started rattling a door, making the whole tank vibrate. A loud, deep, voice blurted, "get off the motherfucking door!" There was a sudden quiet, but a shortlived one, broken first by a racial slur, then an outburst of opposing viewpoints.

We dined alone on paper plates, with a paper spoon, and coffee in a paper cup. All the food was cold, and I just sat and watched the instant potatoes sag away. Part of the lock-up punishment was no sugar, salt, cream or canteen, which made it quite clear that the lock-up section was the real jail, with all the 20th-century refinements and finesse rubbed away.

A trustee came by to collect the dirty plates. As I handed her mine, she slipped me two cigarettes and some help underneath the plate. I caught them in my hand. The woman winked and I winked back. Sparky was doing okay in the dungeon.

I split the match and lit one of my cigarettes, constantly waving it around so the smoke wouldn't billow out the door in a cloud. I only took a few drags, then clinched, once again for the purpose of keeping the smoke and odor at a minimum. I hid the remaining paraphernalia under a roll of toilet paper; a split match, a piece of striker and a butt and a half.

A few minutes later I received my linen and immediately made up my bed. It looked so comfortable and I was con-templating a quick nap, but the "bar rattler" started up again and had a real freaky time of making everybody miserable. I flopped down anyway, and to my surprise, found that the incessant rythmn of the shaking door was actually soothing me to sleep.

When I return from the land of nod the lights were on in the outsider corridor. Time had disappeared completely and I wasn't sure if it was still the same day or the next morning. Tears filled my eyes as I reflected on how low I had come in existence. Not only was I in jail, but I was in a jail that was in the jail! I consoled myself with the fact that at least I would be released from lock-up in the foreseeable future, whereas those women on the other side would live in this hell-hole indefinitely. The thought made me bitter, the idea that there wasn't enough compassion involved with handling the women who couldn't help their actions. I thought about the old lady in church and wondered about her fate.

"Lights out, ladies!" The officer placed a special emphasis on "ladies," indicating she felt the title was really out of place. "There will be no more talking!"

Even the wackos on the other side quieted down. I was thinking about Norma, when Rio's voice started to float down the tier. She was singing "Amazing Grace," and as I lay on my cot an extraordinary sense of peace overtook me. I thought it ludicrous that such beauty and sweetness could thrive in that sickening environment. Perhaps the filth and degradation played a part in making Rio's gentle sound so lovely. When the song ended someone sniffled. It took a moment or two for me to realize that I was the sniffler.

"Night, baby," Sparky said through the quiet.

"Night, Sparky," I said, crawling under the covers. "Night, Rio."

"Beddy bye, Ima."

The noise started again on the other side, which served as a signal for the bar rattler on our side to start up. I slept through it all.

I spent several days in the madness. On the fifth day Sparky and I were notified that we would be getting out. I was relieved, because holding onto reality had become quite a chore. Rio was informed at the same time that she would remain in the hole. The woman who had gotten busted with the reds had also implicated her. When I walked past her cell I felt a heavy weight. I was thankful that I was going back upstairs, but I found it difficult to leave Rio behind. I stopped.

"Well, man . . ." I attempted a grin. "Keep on keeping on . . ."

Rio smiled through the bars. "Aw . . . shit!" She popped her fingers. "Ain't nuttin' but a meatball."

"Come on, Ima, unless you want to stay down here!" I touched Rio's hand, then walked toward the front.

Sparky's door swung next. She danced out onto the tier. As she zipped to the front she hollered at everyone she passed. "Rio, you take care, hear? Things get tight, send me some word."

My pre-trial hearing went painfully slow. Before my trial began, Sparky was long gone to the joint, and Norma was scheduled to follow her on a parole violation. We never discussed her leaving, except for the first time, where we both ended up boo-hooing like two babies. After that, we acted as if her leaving was of no great importance to either of us. I knew I would miss her terribly. However, I learned from Sparky's departure that I would recover. Losing friends was a normal part of pulling time.

The bus from the women's prison always came on Thursday mornings. Norma and I had taken to bickering every Wednesday evening. On Thursdays, we wouldn't even look at each other until the shipment had gone. After a month of this ritual, her name finally appeared on the shipment list.

"Well, baby, this is it." Her expression was cloudy. "You keep everything in the store . . . and take care . . ."

I fought back the tears. "Why don't you take the cash? I'll keep the goodies . . . There's enough to maintain the business . . ."

She agreed, as real money was useful anywhere. I watched in silence while she packed a brown paper bag with necessities; toothbrush, toothpaste, comb and cigarettes. I ached to tell her I would miss her and that I would never forget her as long as I lived, but I knew the spoken words would make all of our defenses crumble.

"You take care of yourself, you hear?" she mumbled, with her head bent over the bag. "Don't let me hear no kinda shit about you either . . ."

"You won't . . . Norma . . .?" I almost choked on my uneven words. Finally, I decided that people shouldn't have to hide the things they felt. "I wish I was going with you!" I blurted.

She looked straight at me, first with the Norma-look I had encountered on our first meeting, but it wouldn't work and she knew it. "Stop talking crazy, dizmo." She smiled lovingly and ruffled my hair, like my mama used to do. "we'll see each other again. You can be with that!"

"All ladies for the bus! Up front! NOW!"

"Well, that's my horse in the chute." She exhaled heavily. "My hair even?" She turned her back to me.

I didn't reach for my usual pat. Instead, I had to wipe the blinding tears away with the back of my hand. Norma peered over her shoulder. She touched my face with her hand.

"Bye, baby . . . You . . ." Her demeanor began to fall apart, but before it did, she snatched up her bag and hurried out. She didn't look back.

I took over as the new trustee, which meant I was the one who swept the tank and performed little odds and ends, in return for a dress with two stripes and a pass to T.V. every night. The remainder of that day when Norma left I stayed in the cell with my face buried in the lousy mystery she had given me on my first day. Mainly, I thought about her and I cried.

I woke the next morning with the realization that it was time to get my head together. I was on my bunk smoking, when a new bunch of bookings came onto the tier. One fish in particular caught my eye, because it was obvious that she had never been in the slammers before. I saw the same frightened look I remembered carrying in with me. I stood up and leaned against my doorway, as B.B began assigning cells. When she came to the young girl, I motioned to have her put in my cell.

The frightened fugitive from juvenile hall walked my way and I scrutinized her closely. This in turn caused her to check herself out, mainly to see if she still had her dress on. I smirked. She jammed her hands into her pockets self-consciously. I pulled out a pack of cigarettes and offered her one. She took it, hesitating, then swallowed hard.

"Hi . . . I'm Alowese . . . Alowese Friggit . . ."

I stepped aside to let her past. "Ima Fibbon here. Come on in and make yourself at home. No sense standing on the freeway, acting like some kinda vagrant . . ."

SOME BEGINNINGS AT THE END

Othello Noel—

Rahway State Prison, New Jersey

Noel is one of those whacked-out cons who would send Sigmund Freud in search of a therapist after a one-hour session. Yet once this wild maniac gets near a canvas, he is a veritable genius. There is a little girl in his life and she will tell you her daddy is just outasight.

WHERE SUNLIGHT FAILS TO
ENTER, A FLOWER IS NEVER
GROWN. WHERE THE LIGHT
OF HUMANITY FADES, SEEDS
OF NEGLECT ARE SOWN.

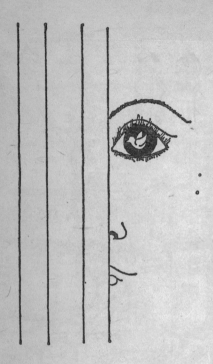

ON SALE WHEREVER PAPERBACKS ARE SOLD
— or use this coupon to order directly from the publisher.

Filled with little-known facts, this comprehensive alphabet of original crime includes some explosive news about the white-washed world of American business, police, and politics.

Mafia Books

Y3472	Pictorial History Of The Mafia $1.95	Don Maclean
T2464	The Mafia 75¢ Ed. Phil Hirsch	
V3311	Mafia: Operation Cocaine $1.25	Don Romano
V3339	Mafia: Operation Hijack $1.25	Don Romano
V2756	The Mafia Don $1.25 G. Ziran	
V3170	Mafia: Operation Porno $1.25	Don Romano
V3444	Mafia: Operation Hit Man $1.25	Don Romano
V3510	MAFIA: Operation Loan Shark $1.25	Don Romano

Send to: PYRAMID PUBLICATIONS,
Dept. M.O., 9 Garden Street, Moonachie, N.J. 07074

NAME

ADDRESS

CITY

STATE   ZIP

I enclose $_____, which includes the total price of all books ordered plus 50¢ per book postage and handling for the first book and 25¢ for each additional. If my total order is $10.00 or more, I understand that Pyramid will pay all postage and handling.
No COD's or stamps. Please allow three to four weeks for delivery.
Prices subject to change.   P-46